THURMAN L. COSS is chairman of the department of philosophy and religion at Hamline University, St. Paul, Minnesota.

Earning his Ph.D. from Drew University in 1952, he then attended the University of Manchester in England on a Fulbright grant. In addition to visiting the continent, Dr. Coss has been to both Jordan and Israel. He has traveled the area where the Dead Sea Scrolls were found, and while tramping the hills of Judea, he and his companion were detained by the Bedouins until they could prove their neutral identity.

A popular and respected instructor on campus, Dr. Coss is also in demand as a lecturer to civic and church groups in the Midwest both in person and on educational television. The enthusiastic response to his talks on the Dead Sea Scrolls led to the effective question-and-answer format used in *Secrets from the Caves*.

Secrets
from the Caves

Secrets
from the Caves

A Layman's Guide to the Dead Sea Scrolls

Thurman L. Coss

Abingdon Press   NEW YORK NASHVILLE

SECRETS FROM THE CAVES

Copyright © 1963 by Abingdon Press

Library of Congress Catalog Card Number: 63-15707

SET UP, PRINTED, AND BOUND BY THE
PARTHENON PRESS, AT NASHVILLE,
TENNESSEE, UNITED STATES OF AMERICA

Dedicated to
BARBARA

Preface

ONE OF MY FOND RECOLLECTIONS OF BYGONE DAYS CARRIES ME back to the main desk and adjoining reading room in the library of an eastern school. The day was warm, final examinations were near, and the students with bowed heads were either sleeping through their volumes or making one last attempt to do what should have been done in an earlier and cooler period.

Without warning, the heavy silence was broken by the soft Scottish lilt of a venerable professor quoting a well-known verse of Scripture. Those who awakened in time heard him say, "Of making many books there is no end, and much study is the weariness of the flesh." It was just the tension reliever that many of us needed, and we returned to our labors with lighter spirits.

The specialist who reads the present volume may rightly conclude that we have here still another treatment of the Dead Sea Scrolls, but I hope that he will note a few differences which may make the present effort worthwhile. First of all, this is a book for lay people. Samuel Sandmel, the well-known Jewish scholar who specializes in the study of the New Testament and is the past president of the Society of Biblical Literature and Exegesis, has just recently remarked that, despite the number of books written about the Dead Sea Scrolls, there are very few which are designed specifically with the lay reader in mind.

7

Millar Burrows of Yale University and Frank Cross, Jr., of Harvard, to name but two of the foremost students of the scrolls, have produced cautious scholarly studies of the scrolls. Admirable as these works are, there are many lay people who lack the knowledge of Hebrew and the knowledge of Hebrew history and religious thought necessary for the understanding of these scholarly volumes. More than once an interested lay person has come to me after a lecture and admitted that he has tried to read one of the more technical studies of the scrolls only to be discouraged by a mass of details incomprehensible to him.

In an attempt to meet the needs of these lay people who want a handy digest and guide to the scrolls, I have adopted a question-and-answer style of writing. This format was first suggested to me by Rabbi Morris Kertzer's book *What Is a Jew?* It is hoped that this catechetical approach will provide a compact and convenient introduction to the scrolls. The questions listed in the table of contents can serve as a quick index to the specific aspects of scrolls study which interest the reader most. Turning to the appropriate page, he can find a brief, nontechnical answer to his question. At least, this is the goal which I set before myself as I begin my work. If I fail, it will be because I have become so "wrapped up" in the scrolls that my own interest is no longer that of the layman. But having had the privilege of introducing people to the scrolls through educational television and dozens of lectures each year, I know that I am raising many of the questions which the nonspecialist is asking. In fact, many of the questions in this book are the very queries directed to me after my formal lectures have ended.

There is a second reason why I write about the scrolls for laymen. As a teacher of Bible in a church-related school, I want my students to know about the scrolls. The time available for the teaching of either the Old Testament or the New Testament is so limited that I feel it is improper procedure to take much time out of the regular class periods for a consideration of this important but specialized topic. I write, therefore, with my students in mind and hope that through the medium of these pages they may begin to share the enthusiasm of their instructor for these ancient documents.

By way of acknowledgments, I would first express my gratitude to Paul H. Giddens, president of Hamline University, who granted the sabbatical leave and made the actual writing of this book possible. He has even taken time across the years to supply me with clippings of articles on the Dead Sea Scrolls which have come to his attention. For all this assistance, I am most grateful.

Secondly, I thank the American Zionist Committee and the Inter-University Committee on Israel for making it possible for me to visit Israel. While I was at the Hebrew University in Jerusalem, I not only saw many of the important scrolls but also had the opportunity to discuss them with a number of leading Jewish scholars. For this experience, I am especially indebted to Rabbi Isaiah Zeldin of Beverly Hills, California, Rabbi David Greenberg of New York City, and Fred Fingerote of Los Angeles.

Several institutions have helped me in various ways. The University of California at Los Angeles permitted me to come and go freely through its stacks. The First Methodist Church of Santa Monica provided the office for the actual writing of this manuscript, and several groups within this church have listened to my lectures on the scrolls. The staff of the Santa Monica Public Library supplied me with microfilm copies of the *New York Times*. John Pepin of Drew University made it possible for me to live on the Drew campus during one summer and use the resources of that institution. I have also found needed books and periodicals in the libraries of Luther Theological Seminary at St. Paul and Fuller Theological Seminary of Pasadena. Apart from such generous assistance, I could not have completed my work.

My debt to individuals is so great that I cannot thank them all for their contributions, but I would mention a few who

9

have rendered special services to me. Jonas Greenfield of U.C.L.A. supplied an English translation of some French resource material which he had in his possession. Willard F. Libby and Gordon Ferguson of U.C.L.A. talked with me about the latest developments in the radiocarbon dating process. John Curtis of the First Methodist Church in Santa Monica provided me with photostatic copies of technical articles on infrared radiation and radiocarbon dating. My former student, Miss Beverly Kaemmer, has read the rough draft of this book and made suggestions about grammar and style. Mrs. Brita Allan of the Hamline University Staff has done much of the typing, and four Hamline students, Lucille Livermore, Susan Merritt, Carol Townsend, and Gary Miller, have worked patiently with me in the reading of galleys and page proofs.

If it be not presumptuous, I would like to mention with the warmest of thanks those teachers who introduced me to theology and biblical studies. To Horton, May, and Kepler of Oberlin, who started me along the way; to Paterson, Craig, and Lewis of Drew, who continued the instruction; to Rowley, Manson, and Gray of the University of Manchester, who made my stay in England rich and rewarding; to Terrien and Grant of Union Theological Seminary, with whom I studied the Psalms and the Fourth Gospel; to all these, I express my deep appreciation. Whatever merit this book may have is due in large part to the excellent teaching and scholarly examples of these gentlemen.

THURMAN L. COSS

Contents

11

CONTENTS

13

X. A Scientific Postscript

Appendix

Bibliography

I

Discovering the Dead Sea Scrolls

What Are the Dead Sea Scrolls?

THE "DEAD SEA SCROLLS" IS A POPULAR TITLE GIVEN TO A SERIES of manuscripts found in caves in the general vicinity of the Dead Sea. At least one scholar has objected that the name is inappropriate because these famous scrolls were not, after all, found pickled in the brine of that famous body of water. This argument notwithstanding, the popular title remains. In fact the brilliant journalist Edmund Wilson, who made the scrolls famous, still gives his book on the subject the ambiguous if not inaccurate title, *The Scrolls from the Dead Sea.*

In the early days, when only one cave was known to have produced manuscripts, the title "Dead Sea Scrolls" naturally applied exclusively to those scrolls which came from what we now call "Cave I." Now that we know that a total of eleven caves at one site and two caves at another site have produced manuscript material, it is necessary to broaden the title to include all these discoveries. In our present study we shall be concerned primarily with the scrolls from the eleven caves of Qumran, but we shall make occasional references to the four caves of Murabbaat (two of which produced inscribed materials).[1]

---

[1] For the sake of completeness, we should mention here that some caves of unknown location, probably south of Murabbaat, have produced manuscript material, as has another site known as Khirbet Mird.

Where Were They Found?

The Dead Sea Scrolls were discovered in a series of caves which are located in the marl cliffs along the northwestern shore of the Dead Sea. Many of the scrolls came from caves near a site known as Qumran.

Qumran is located about seven or eight miles south of modern Jericho. The barrenness of this wasteland of Judea is certainly awesome to one who has been reared in the rich farming area of the midwestern United States. The rays of the summer sun beat mercilessly upon the heads of tourists, and one looks in vain for shade trees at Qumran. We marvel at the thought of people living in this hot and arid climate, but this is precisely what the people of the scrolls did. Father de Vaux, a French priest and archaeologist who has played a leading role in the scrolls drama, says that he himself has spent many weeks and months living in this area while excavations of Khirbet Qumran (a khirbet is a ruin) were in process. He agrees that it is not the most pleasant way to live, but disagrees with Del Medico, another writer on the subject of the scrolls, who claims that permanent residence in this area is highly unlikely, if indeed not impossible.

There would be no rain in this area during the summer months. Temperatures might easily rise above ninety degrees Fahrenheit. The numerous caves in the marl cliffs would provide shade and living quarters, but this is certainly not the kind of comfort to which Westerners have become accustomed. Only disciplined men would choose to leave Jerusalem and make this site their home: in our case, men who were at odds with the Jerusalem priesthood and determined to carve out an existence for God's elect here in the wilderness of Judea.

A second group of scrolls was discovered in some caves situated in cliffs which overlook the Wadi Murabbaat. This wadi, or valley, is about twelve miles southwest of Qumran as the crow flies (and this, by all odds, is the easiest way of traversing these hills of Judea). The distance of Murabbaat from Jerusalem is approximately seventeen miles in a southeasterly direction.

According to the British scholar Allegro, the caves of Murabbaat would thrill even the more seasoned and experienced of spelunkers or cave explorers.[2] They are located in the north side of an almost vertical cliff which provides one wall for a gorge six hundred to eight hundred feet deep. The caves are Gargantuan in comparison with those of Qumran. (Cave I at Qumran measures approximately twenty-five feet long, seven feet wide, and eight or nine feet in height.) One of them is almost two hundred feet long, twenty feet wide, and the same in height. Allegro tells how G. Lankester Harding, who was then Director of Antiquities for Jordan, along with a member of the Taamirah tribe, decided to investigate one of the caves. All was going reasonably well until suddenly and without any warning the Bedouin who was in the lead dropped out of sight. After a few anxious moments, Harding was relieved to hear the voice of his companion. The paraffin flare which the Bedouin had been carrying was relighted and a slightly shaken native scrambled out of the pit into which he had fallen.

While there is no direct connection between the scrolls and documents of Murabbaat and those more famous scrolls from Qumran, they are all grouped together here under the popular title "Dead Sea Scrolls."

Why Have the Dead Sea Scrolls Awakened Such Great Interest Among Laymen?

There can be no doubt that credit for exciting the American people about the scrolls must go to Edmund Wilson, a layman in the field of biblical scholarship but a proven master in the

[2] For an exciting account of the work at Murabbaat, see J. M. Allegro, *The Dead Sea Scrolls* (Harmondsworth: Penguin Books Ltd., 1956), pp. 168-79.

art of writing. In an article appearing in the May, 1955, issue of the *New Yorker,* Wilson introduced the American public to the amazing discoveries and even more amazing scrolls from the cave on the northwestern side of the Dead Sea. Wilson told his story in such an engaging manner that the May issue of the *New Yorker* was soon sold out. His book, which was published in the same year, became a best seller, and soon the Dead Sea Scrolls were challenging politics and the weather as sources of popular conversations. Lectures were demanded by the public; television programs dramatized the discovery of the scrolls; scholarly books on the subject were purchased at a surprising rate. Recently, I was forced to search for a larger lecture hall to accommodate an unexpectedly large audience who wanted to know more about the Dead Sea Scrolls.

It was not, however, the clever use of the pen alone which aroused the popular interest in the scrolls. In his article and in his book, Wilson left the impression that both Christians and Jews were reluctant to study the scrolls lest some of their preconceptions in matters of religion be upset. He seemed to suggest that the essence of Christianity was to be found in doctrines and ideas which had developed naturally and gradually over a period of two hundred years. To find supposedly unique Christian ideas in pre-Christian literature must certainly disturb the devout. At such a time only the uncommitted could deal objectively with the Dead Sea Scrolls.

Wilson hinted that New Testament scholars were afraid of the scrolls and had "almost without exception boycotted the whole subject of the scrolls." [3] Such remarks naturally aroused the curiosity of lay people, and they wanted to know more about these rolls of leather. If traditional Christianity were being threatened by the recent discoveries, the lay people wanted to be informed.

[3] Edmund Wilson, *The Scrolls from the Dead Sea* (New York: Meridian Books, Inc., 1959), p. 99.

Who Found the Dead Sea Scrolls?

A seminomadic Bedouin by the name of Muhammad adh-Dhib found the scrolls. He was a member of the Taamirah tribe. Early accounts of Muhammad's discovery mentioned contraband goods, customs officers with guns, and a consequent flight of Taamirah Bedouins which resulted in Muhammad's being in the area of Qumran. Fleeing from the law, he had come by chance upon Cave I and its treasures.

While this makes an interesting story, it appears to have one fault: It is not true. A more accurate version is that of G. Lankester Harding, who personally talked to Muhammad about the discovery. According to Harding, Muhammad and a friend had been pasturing their flock in the vicinity of Qumran. One of the flock, either a goat or a sheep, strayed away and the boys went in search of it. Noticing a small hole in the side of the marl cliff, the curious boys pulled themselves up to the opening and threw a rock inside. Instead of the dull thud they had expected, they heard what seemed to be the shattering of an unknown object.

For one reason or another, the boys did not investigate immediately. But they could not forget the strange sound, and returned the next day for a more thorough investigation. The entrance into this cave was so small that it was probably necessary for one boy to wriggle and squirm while the other boy offered a little added push. Once inside, they were rewarded for their efforts. There on the floor of the cave were eight large jars varying slightly in size but averaging about two feet in height and ten inches in diameter. Seven of the jars were empty, but the eighth contained the treasure. From this jar, the boys pulled out one large leather scroll and two smaller ones. This was Cave I at Qumran and the beginning of an exciting episode in the history of archaeology and biblical study. Though we are not certain, it seems likely that Muhammad and his friend had already discovered the large scroll of

Isaiah, the Manual of Discipline, and the Habakkuk Commentary.[4]

When Were They Discovered?

If this question had been asked in 1955, an unqualified and straightforward answer could have been given. And that answer would have been, 1947. This still seems to be the most likely date, but a letter based upon a 1956 interview with Muhammad adh-Dhib has appeared in the *Journal of Near Eastern Studies,* and contradicts the commonly held view of a 1947 discovery. In this interview, Muhammad stated he found the scrolls in 1945 while tending a flock of fifty-five head. Ordinarily he would have counted his flock each evening, but on this particular occasion he had not counted the flock for two days and when he did make the count, he discovered that one goat was missing.

Leaving his own flock with two fellow herdsmen, Muhammad started a search which eventually brought him to a cave with an opening at the top "like a cistern." After throwing his stones and hearing the breaking of jars, Muhammad immediately went inside the cave, where he found ten jars. He broke nine of these with his shepherd's staff and found nothing. When he broke the tenth jar, however, he found the leathers. For a moment, he was uncertain what to do with the scrolls; but remembering that he and his companions needed straps for repairing their sandals, he wrapped up the scrolls in his cloak and carried them away on his back.

After sharing some of the leather with his needy friends, Muhammad took the remainder of the scrolls to his home, where he kept them in a skin bag for more than two years. Finally, an uncle saw the scrolls and suggested that Muhammad contact an antiquities dealer in Bethlehem. This, according to Muhammad, is the story of the discovery.

[4] D. Barthélemy and J. T. Milik, *Discoveries in the Judaean Desert I, Qumran Cave I* (Oxford: Clarendon Press, 1955), p. 5.

One's first reaction is to accept this report. Surely Muhammad would know when he discovered the scrolls. But would he? A more thoughtful evaluation of Muhammad's report raises some interesting questions. Why was Muhammad more precise about details in his 1956 interview than he was in his much earlier report to Harding? Did he really use such old, weak leather for repairing his sandals? Would a semi-Bedouin store in a skin bag for two years what were to him almost worthless leathers, especially when he needed the bag for other purposes? And why would he be bothered carrying old scrolls up and down the hills of Judea when he lived the life of a shepherd and a seminomad? Would it not have been easier and more satisfying to show the scrolls immediately to a Bethlehem dealer in antiquities and get his opinion about their value? [5]

Such questions can be raised without questioning the honesty of Muhammad. Remembering dates is not so important to a Bedouin as it is to Western scholars writing history. Still, there is the haunting possibility that Muhammad's later account may have truth in it. It is the qualification that we keep in mind as we say that the scrolls were discovered in 1947.

What Did Muhammad and His Friends Do with Their Scrolls?

If a degree of uncertainty clouds the exact date of the discovery of the scrolls, even more uncertainty surrounds the handling of the scrolls between the time when they were first found and the time weeks, and even months, later when the scrolls were purchased by men who lived in either Bethlehem or Jerusalem. It seems that Muhammad and his companions offered their leathers to a Bethlehem antiquities dealer. The

[5] For Muhammad's report see W. H. Brownlee, "Muhammad ed-Deeb's Own Story of His Discovery," *Journal of Near Eastern Studies*, XVI (1957), 236-39. J. C. Trever gives a critical evaluation of Muhammad's story in "When Was Qumran Cave I Discovered?" *Revue de Qumran*, February, 1961, pp. 135-41. It is Trever who raises most of the questions listed above. Cf. Brownlee, "Edh-Dheeb's Story of His Scroll Discovery," *Revue de Qumran*, October, 1962, pp. 483-94, for further evaluation of this problem.

dealer refused to purchase the scrolls and sent the Bedouins to another Bethlehem merchant, Khalil Eskander Shahin (or Kando).

Kando was also hesitant about buying leathers of unknown value. He urged the Bedouins to take their scrolls to a friend of his in Jerusalem, a George Isaiah, who along with Kando was a member of the Syrian Orthodox Church. Isaiah, in turn, decided that the metropolitan of his church, Athanasius Samuel of St. Mark's Monastery, should see these scrolls.

To shorten a story, the details of which at best are vague, Samuel finally succeeded in purchasing five rolls from the Bedouins. It is likely that these five rolls later proved to be four scrolls, one of which existed in two parts, but even this is debated among the scholars. The exact purchase price for this lot of scrolls is not known, but all the rumored prices which have come to my attention indicate that the figure was less than two hundred dollars, and even this may be an exaggerated figure.

Athanasius Samuel tells us that he first heard about these scrolls, described by a Jerusalem merchant as being wrapped "like mummies," in the month of Nisan (April in our calendar), 1947. When Samuel saw the scrolls, he realized that their language was foreign to him. He did burn a piece of one of the scrolls and decided on the basis of the resulting odor that the scrolls were leather. Beyond this he had little idea about the nature or worth of the scrolls. He would have to seek the advice of experts before he knew whether his purchase had been wise.

Meantime, more scrolls had been sold to another dealer. Samuel says that this dealer was a Jewish merchant, but there is some evidence for believing that the buyer of this second portion of scrolls was Deidi Salahi, an antiquities dealer in Bethlehem who would later sell his scrolls to E. L. Sukenik of the Hebrew University in Jerusalem. Athanasius Samuel now complains that he would have purchased this second lot of scrolls had it not been for the mistake of one of his own priests, Father Boulos, who failed to recognize that the Bedouin salesmen who appeared at the door of St. Mark's Monastery were selling scrolls that Samuel wanted to buy. When Boulos sent the Bedouins away, they may have taken their portion of the scrolls back to Bethlehem and sold them there to an antiquities dealer. It may be this group of scrolls which was later purchased by Sukenik, but we must point out that conjecture is involved in this conclusion.[6]

Who Was the First Person to Recognize the Antiquity and Value of the Scrolls?

There is no doubt about the correct answer to this question. E. L. Sukenik, professor of archaeology at the Hebrew University in Jerusalem, must be accorded this honor. Yigael Yadin, son of the late Sukenik, certainly speaks accurately when he says, "It was my father . . . who first recognized the antiquity and the significance of the scrolls." [7] It was, indeed, Sukenik who not only identified the Isaiah scroll but recognized that this manuscript was at least one thousand years older than any previously known Hebrew copy of this same book. In an age when faked documents have often fooled the experts, Sukenik's conclusions, made late in the year 1947 and now confirmed by both archaeological and paleographical (paleography is a comparative study of ancient scripts) evidence, remain as a fitting tribute to the wisdom and sound judgment of this scholar.

One of the most exciting exercises in the study of the scrolls is the reading of excerpts from the diary of E. L. Sukenik.[8] From

[6] Cf. Mar Athanasius Y. Samuel, "The Purchase of the Jerusalem Scrolls," *Biblical Archaeologist* XII (1949), 26-31.

[7] Yigael Yadin, *The Message of the Scrolls* (New York: Simon & Schuster, 1957), pp. 12, 16. Yadin, a former general in Israel's army, is also a highly competent archaeologist.

[8] E. L. Sukenik, ed., *The Dead Sea Scrolls of the Hebrew University* (Jerusalem: The Magnes Press of the Hebrew University, 1955), p. 17. Cf. Yadin, *Message of the Scrolls,* pp. 16-25.

these excerpts we discover that Sukenik first learned about the scrolls on November 25, 1947. He had returned only recently from a leave of absence and a lecture tour in the United States. When he went to his office on Sunday, November 23, he found a note from a well-known Jerusalem antiquities dealer asking Sukenik to meet him as soon as possible.

It was on Tuesday that Sukenik went to see the dealer. When he arrived, he was told a story about a Hebrew scroll which had been found in a jar. Immediately, Sukenik wondered if someone had found a genizah (a storage place for worn and defective scrolls). Two days later, Sukenik again visited the Armenian merchant and saw four pieces of leather inscribed in a Hebrew script which seemed to Sukenik to be "very much like the writing on the Uzziah inscription," a script which scholars usually date in either the first century B.C. or the first century A.D. Was it possible that in the twentieth century inscribed material would come to light, inscribed material that was perhaps two thousand years old? This was the question which was to arouse odd and exciting thoughts in the mind of Sukenik.

On November 29, 1947, Sukenik risked the dangers of travel in a country that seemed perilously close to an outbreak of hostilities and went to Bethlehem to see more scrolls. While in Bethlehem, Sukenik also saw two jars which had supposedly come from the scrolls cave. Sukenik took them home with him. After more study of the rolls of leather, Sukenik made this entry in his diary for December 1, 1947: "I read a little more in the 'parchments.' I'm afraid of going too far in thinking about them. It may be that this is one of the greatest finds ever made in Palestine, a find we never so much as hoped for." At the end of this year, recalling in sadness the death of his son who had been lost in action while serving as a fighter pilot, Sukenik remarked, "Were it not for the *genizah,* the year would have been intolerable for me." [9]

[9] Sukenik, *op. cit.,* p. 17.

As a result of his November and December meetings with the dealers and the consequent reading and study of the script of the scrolls (those scrolls which could be opened easily without damaging them), Sukenik recognized the antiquity of these finds and purchased them for the Hebrew University. There were six bundles in his original lot, but we now know that these six bundles represented three scrolls. Sukenik had purchased an Isaiah scroll, a scroll of Thanksgiving Psalms (there were four parts to this crumpled scroll), and another roll of leather which we now call popularly the War scroll, but which is more accurately entitled "The War of the Sons of Light with the Sons of Darkness." These three scrolls are sometimes referred to as the Hebrew University scrolls in order to distinguish them from those bought by Athanasius Samuel of St. Mark's Monastery.

What Did Athanasius Samuel Do with His Scrolls?

He sought expert advice in an attempt to identify and establish the value of his scrolls. In response to one of Samuel's requests for a scholarly opinion of his scrolls, Father van der Ploeg, a visiting Dutch scholar at the École Biblique in Jerusalem, came to St. Mark's Monastery and identified one of the leather rolls as an Isaiah scroll. Father van der Ploeg may have been the first person to identify any of the scrolls, but even Father van der Ploeg failed to recognize the great antiquity of this scroll.

Samuel also turned for advice to Stephen Hannah Stephan, a member of his church who was employed by the Jordanian Department of Antiquities and was working at the Palestine Archaeological Museum as an assistant librarian. Stephen thought the scrolls were of no value and did not inform his superiors about what he had seen. (It is unfortunate that G. Lankester Harding, Jordan's Director of Antiquities, was not informed about the discovery of these scrolls until November, 1948, when he received word via an April publication of the

Bulletin of the American Schools of Oriental Research, which carried notices about the scrolls.)

Samuel was discouraged by Stephan's advice not to pay "even one shilling for them," but was still unwilling to give up. I cannot tell in detail of Samuel's search for guidance and advice. Suffice it to say that a Jewish journalist and two representatives of the Hebrew University looked at the St. Mark's scrolls and failed to recognize their antiquity. Samuel's own patriarch in Syria admitted ignorance about such matters and recommended that Samuel go to the American University of Beirut. Unfortunately, the professor of Hebrew at the American University was on vacation and not available for an opinion, so Samuel had to return home momentarily thwarted in his attempt to learn more about his leathers.

All this was happening during the months of July, August, September, and October. There is some evidence that during this same period someone associated with St. Mark's Monastery encouraged the organization of illegal excavation parties which ransacked Cave I, destroyed valuable archaeological evidence, and perhaps recovered more scrolls and/or fragments. The identity of the guilty ones is not known for certain.

By December, Sukenik learned of the St. Mark's scrolls. Thinking that they probably belonged to the same cache which had produced the scrolls he had been studying, he made an attempt to visit St. Mark's Monastery. The unsettled condition in the country at that time made this proposed visit impossible, and it was not until late January that Sukenik received the welcome invitation to meet a certain Anton Kiraz, who promised to bring the St. Mark's scrolls with him so that Sukenik could look at them.

As soon as Sukenik saw this lot of scrolls his surmise was confirmed. He identified the large Isaiah scroll immediately and recognized that the other scrolls, like those he had purchased for the Hebrew University, were both ancient and valuable. Sukenik was granted permission to take three of these scrolls home for further study. According to agreement, Sukenik returned the scrolls to Kiraz on February 6, 1948, and indicated a willingness to buy them. Kiraz promised Sukenik that when the scrolls were put up for sale Sukenik would have the first opportunity to purchase them, but much to Sukenik's disappointment he never saw the scrolls again.

Not long after Kiraz's last meeting with Sukenik, the Metropolitan Samuel decided to consult the scholars at the American School of Oriental Research in Jerusalem for their opinion and help. Whereas Kiraz may have had Samuel's permission to show the scrolls to Sukenik, he did not have authority to sell them to Sukenik. Kiraz had left the impression with Sukenik that he and Samuel were joint owners of the scrolls, but Samuel has always denied Kiraz's claim and accordingly made his own inquiries at the American School.

Who Was the First American to See the Scrolls?

John Trever, who is now a professor at Baldwin-Wallace College in Berea, Ohio, was the first American to see any of the Dead Sea Scrolls. Trever's account of this important episode in his life is as lively reading as that found in the excerpts from Sukenik's diary.[10] It was Wednesday afternoon, February 18, 1948, that Omar, the cook at the American School of Oriental Research, went to Trever's room and told him there was a telephone call from Father Butros Sowmy of St. Mark's Monastery. Sowmy informed Trever that he was seeking information about some old manuscripts and wondered if the American could help him.

Trever, who was both a trained student of the Bible and an accomplished photographer of ancient biblical manuscripts, was immediately interested in this story about old scrolls, and he invited Father Sowmy to bring the manuscripts to the American School. On Thursday afternoon Father Sowmy and

[10] J. C. Trever, "The Discovery of the Scrolls," *Biblical Archaeologist* XI (1948), 46-57.

his brother Ibrahim came to the school carrying a small suitcase containing the scrolls. As Trever studied the script of the largest scroll and compared it with that of the Nash Papyrus,[11] a photograph of which he had in his own private collection, he noted a striking similarity. Was it possible that the script on Sowmy's scroll was as old as that on the Nash Papyrus? If so, the scroll he had just unrolled on his bed might be older than the time of Jesus.

"Sleep," says Trever, "was almost impossible that night." Trever knew he had been looking at an Isaiah scroll, but it was the script that really haunted him. If he was correct, this would easily be the oldest Hebrew manuscript of Isaiah in existence.

On Friday, February 20, Trever gained permission from Samuel to photograph his scrolls, and on Saturday the actual work of photographing began. The task was completed by Tuesday of the next week and Trever dispatched some of the photographs to William Foxwell Albright of Johns Hopkins University. It was most reassuring to Trever to receive on March 15 an airmail letter from this acknowledged authority in matters of archaeology and paleography with these words in it:

My heartiest congratulations on the greatest manuscript discovery of modern times! There is no doubt in my mind that the script is more archaic than that of the Nash Papyrus . . . I should prefer a date around 100 B.C. . . . What an absolutely incredible find! And there can happily not be the slightest doubt in the world about the genuineness of the manuscript.[12]

Assured of the antiquity and genuineness of the St. Mark's scrolls, Trever, his companion William Brownlee, and their

[11] The Nash Papyrus is a fragment of a pre-Christian document which is now commonly regarded as coming from either the second or first century B.C. This fragment, inscribed in Hebrew, contains the Ten Commandments, and the Shema of Deut. 6:4-5.

[12] Cf. John Trever's article "Discovery of the Scrolls" cited above.

teacher, Millar Burrows of Yale—Burrows had been on a short vacation in Iraq when the scrolls were first brought to the American School—devoted the rest of their school year to the study of the Dead Sea Scrolls which had come to their attention. The world of biblical scholarship would soon hear about the strange and unexpected discovery of scrolls in a cave located on the northwestern side of the Dead Sea.

What Are the Original Dead Sea Scrolls?

Since all the original scrolls have now been opened, they can here be listed and something told about their physical dimensions in their present state. However, a more detailed introduction to these scrolls must be reserved for the third chapter. First are the scrolls acquired by the Metropolitan, Athanasius Samuel, and later photographed by Trever:

(1) The large *St. Mark's Isaiah scroll* is one foot wide and twenty-four feet long. There is a total of fifty-four columns, representing every chapter in the present book of Isaiah. This is by far the largest of the original Dead Sea Scrolls.

(2) The *Manual of Discipline,* so-called because Burrows suggested that its contents were similar to those that one would expect to find in the Discipline of The Methodist Church, averages about ten inches in width and is six feet long. There are eleven columns in this scroll.

(3) Another of Samuel's scrolls is the *Habakkuk Commentary.* It is five-and-one-half inches wide and about five feet long. There are thirteen columns of text and commentary.

(4) One of Samuel's scrolls, called the *Lamech scroll* because some of the first scholars to see it were able to read the name Lamech on a detached piece of the roll, was so tightly rolled that it defied all early attempts to unroll it. When the scholars and technicians

finally succeeded in opening it (see chap. three), they found the remnants of a scroll about one foot wide and nine-and-one-quarter feet long containing a total of twenty-two columns.

In addition to these four major scrolls, Samuel also had some fragments of Daniel which are small but important because they may be separated by less than a century from the original edition of the biblical book of Daniel. It may be that these fragments came from the clandestine operations of the treasure hunters who ransacked Cave I.

(5) Two of the scrolls purchased by Sukenik for the Hebrew University were in a very poor state of preservation. The *Thanksgiving Psalms scroll* came to Sukenik as three separate sheets and a fourth bundle of some seventy fragments. Each separate sheet measures about twelve-and-one-half inches by twenty-three-and-one-half inches. The original of this scroll may have been more than nine feet long and included as many as forty Psalms.

(6) The *Hebrew University Isaiah scroll* is also in a poor state of preservation. The folds of the leather stuck together in such fashion that this scroll was not opened until the summer of 1949. Thirty-nine of the sixty-six chapters of the book of Isaiah are represented in this scroll, but many of these chapters are represented only by small fragments. The largest sheet preserved measures about one-and-one-half feet by eight inches. The writing of this scroll is so faded that infrared photography was essential before the text could be deciphered.

(7) The third scroll purchased by Sukenik is in the best condition. This *War scroll* measures about six inches in width and nine-and-one-half feet in length. Four large sheets contain eighteen columns, and a remnant

of a fifth sheet shows that the original scroll had at least nineteen columns.

These seven scrolls are, then, the original Dead Sea Scrolls. Many more scrolls were to be found in the next ten years, and for that story we go now to our second chapter.

More Discoveries and Homes
for the Scrolls

When Was Cave I Officially Excavated?

THE OFFICIAL EXCAVATION OF CAVE I WAS CARRIED OUT between February 15 and March 5, 1949. The delay in examining this cave, which had produced valuable scrolls almost two years earlier, must be seen in light of the circumstances which prevailed. First, as I have already noted, no one thought to inform the Director of Antiquities about the discoveries. It was not until late in 1948 that Harding learned about the scrolls, and then the political situation in Jordan was in such a state of unrest that it was not easy to organize an archaeological expedition to the Dead Sea area. Moreover, those people who had been involved in illegal operations (illegal because antiquities belong to the country in which they are found) were understandably quiet about the exact location of the cave.

Cave I was discovered officially by soldiers in January of 1949. The official excavation crew began its work on February 15. Harding and Father de Vaux supervised the work. Using small brushes, tweezers, penknives, and fingers, the workers began to sort out from the dust of the cave and the debris left outside the cave by the earlier treasure hunters the hundreds of inscribed fragments of leather and papyrus. Sometimes there would be as little as one half a letter on a fragment, but everything was saved. This is the way of trained archaeologists. Today's seemingly insignificant shred may be tomorrow's clue to a mystery.

What Did the Excavators Find?

They found linen cloth which had been used for scroll wrappers, jars with covers (all the jars had been broken but the pieces remained and could be fitted together), a bowl and a pot, a pitcher, two fragments of a wooden comb, and parts of three phylacteries (little leathers containing scriptural verses worn on the head and left arm by some Jews when they pray). The clay of the jars seems now to be from the Roman period, and it is at least possible that the linen cloth was a local product of Palestine in the first century A.D. Thus we begin to accumulate evidence for dating the scrolls.

Inscribed fragments of several biblical books were found, including Genesis, Leviticus, Deuteronomy, Judges, I and II Samuel, Isaiah, Ezekiel, and Psalms. There were also examples of nonbiblical works such as commentaries, apocryphal books, liturgical texts, and collections of hymns. At least a few of these additional fragments appear to belong to some of the original Dead Sea Scrolls such as the War scroll, the Manual of Discipline, and the Thanksgiving Psalms, thus further confirming that the original Dead Sea Scrolls did indeed come from this very cave.

Even the rubble heap left at the mouth of Cave I produced valuable material. Instead of keeping every fragment of material as the archaeologists would, the earlier unskilled treasure hunters had discarded many pieces that seemed worthless to them. When this fact became obvious to the official team, every cubic inch of earth was searched carefully and many additional fragments were recovered.

Unfortunately, the personal habits of the earlier amateur archaeologists provided clues which helped identify them. As they went about their work, they dropped cigarette stubs, pieces of modern newspapers, and—most revealing of all—a cigarette roller bearing the owner's name. In light of such evidence, one needed no degree in archaeology to guess the identity of at least one visitor to the cave. If the modern reports on this episode are accurate, we should not blame the Bedouins for these illicit operations, but rather, we should look toward Jerusalem and St. Mark's Monastery.

Have Other Caves at Qumran Been Examined and Excavated?

As a result of the friendly competition between the Bedouins and the archaeologists, hundreds of crevices and caves were examined during the period from 1949 to 1956. Often the Bedouins won the game and came away with the booty; sometimes the archaeologists got there first.

It was late in February, 1952, that the archaeologists received word that the Bedouins had discovered another fragment-bearing cave at Qumran. Leaving their work at Murabbaat (to be described below), the archaeologists hastened back to the Qumran area and initiated a systematic search for caves and manuscripts. Combing an area five miles long on the northwestern side of the Dead Sea, the workmen scaled the cliffs and examined almost three hundred caves and crevices. About forty of these caves indicated human habitation sometime in the past, and twenty-five of them produced pottery of the same type that had been found in Cave I.

Cave II, which the Bedouins had already found, was rediscovered and investigated between March 10 and March 29, 1952. In spite of the fact that this cave contained fragments representing as many as one hundred manuscripts, including Exodus, Leviticus, Numbers, Deuteronomy, Jeremiah, Psalms, and Ruth, the specialists who evaluate these matters agree that Cave II finds are unspectacular in comparison with those of other caves and sites.

On March 14, the archaeologists won a round from the Bedouins and found Cave III. This cave was located about one mile north of Cave I. The roof of Cave III had collapsed, but the persistent efforts of the diggers brought unexpected rewards. This was the cave of the copper scrolls. Lying up against one of the side walls were two metal scrolls, one considerably larger than the other. The advanced state of oxidation and the brittle condition of these odd rolls made it impossible for the finders to unroll them immediately. Indeed, the problem of opening the copper scrolls would perplex the experts for several years. All that could be done at the moment was to coat the scrolls with a paraffin wax to prevent crumbling. The scrolls were then moved to the Palestine Archaeological Museum, where they were to remain for three years. Meantime, the hypotheses and conjectures about the contents of the copper scrolls flowed freely.

What Is the Partridge Cave?

The partridge cave is really Cave IV at Qumran. It was discovered by the Bedouins in September of 1952. As Father Milik tells the story, the Bedouins found this cave after listening to one of their venerable graybeards tell of following a wounded partridge into a cave and finding there an old terra-cotta lamp and a few potsherds. Excited by the hope that they might discover a new treasure trove, the Bedouins took ropes and provisions and set out once more for the Qumran area. By this time the Bedouins knew the value of scrolls and fragments, knew that a square inch of inscribed material might bring as much as eighteen dollars' reward. Scrambling up cliffs and dangling by ropes may not be easy, but when the rewards are this high, cave searching becomes both more exciting and more lucrative than herding goats.

Once more, their efforts were rewarded. They found a very small hole in an almost vertical cliff of the wadi that cuts the plateau upon which the ruins of Qumran are located. The archaeologists had been excavating Qumran earlier in this same year and had not noticed this small opening, but the Bedouins, guided by the story of the partridge cave, were not to be deprived. Their sharp eyes spotted the entrance and they began excavation immediately. After turning over a few cubic yards of earth, they found treasure in the form of a compact layer containing literally thousands of manuscript fragments. In the words of Frank Cross of Harvard, this collection of fragments is "unrivaled in its size and import." [1]

Exercising caution and care in the handling of their fragments, the Bedouins packed them into cigarette boxes, old film boxes, and other available containers. They worked in relays to complete their work as quickly as possible, and soon their discoveries were being offered for sale in Jerusalem. Father de Vaux was approached and was able to purchase one group of fragments for £1,300, or approximately $3,600.

Father de Vaux informed G. Lankester Harding about these fragments, and the Director of Antiquities made immediate plans to return to the Dead Sea. Between September 22 and September 29, the archaeologists made their official excavation of Cave IV and found additional hundreds of fragments which the Bedouins had either missed or had not had time to reach. In terms of the number of manuscripts represented, this was to be the richest of the cave discoveries.

The very wealth of fragments proved to be an embarrassment. Both the French school, with which Father de Vaux was associated, and the Palestine Archaeological Museum had almost exhausted their financial resources buying earlier fragments from Murabbaat and other caves. Where would the authorities turn for the money needed to redeem these treasures from the Bedouins?

Harding went first to the government of Jordan and was granted £15,000 (more than $42,000), but this was soon used and more was needed. Jordan could not spare more money but she was willing to sell the scrolls. Any learned institution which

[1] Frank M. Cross, Jr., *The Ancient Library of Qumran and Modern Biblical Studies* (rev. ed.; Garden City, N. Y.: Doubleday & Co., Inc., 1961), p. 34. For Milik's account see his *Ten Years of Discovery in the Wilderness of Judea*, trans. J. Strugnell (London: S. C. M. Press, 1959), pp. 16-17.

could pay cash immediately to "save the scrolls" would receive a specified portion of these fragments after they had been sorted and published.

McGill University was the first institution to offer financial assistance. Helped by a widow who wanted the scrolls to be given to McGill in honor of her husband, McGill made available $15,000. Manchester University subscribed about $2,800. The Vatican Library offered several thousand dollars, as did the University of Heidelberg. McCormick Theological Seminary of Evanston, Illinois, was the first institution in the United States to buy some of the scrolls. Then, in 1958, the *New York Times* for September 19 announced that the All Souls Unitarian Church of New York City had acquired a portion of the scrolls in the form of the earliest Hebrew copy of the Ten Commandments. The reported price was "several thousand dollars."

By this time, the reader may be curious about the contents of Cave IV. More than 380 manuscripts from this cave have already been identified. Of this number, about one hundred biblical manuscripts have been identified thus far, including every book in the Hebrew Bible with the one exception of Esther. Cross believes that Cave IV finds may represent the library of the people of Qumran.

Many of us have undoubtedly studied a friend's library to see what his tastes in reading are. We may find that he favors theology and religion or perhaps the latest in scientific discoveries—hopefully some of each. In similar fashion, it is interesting to note the reading preferences of the Qumran sectarians. Judging from the number of copies of a given manuscript found there, these Jews had a decided predilection for Deuteronomy, Isaiah, Psalms, and the minor prophets (Hosea, Joel, Amos, Obadiah, Jonah, Micah, Nahum, Habakkuk, Zephaniah, Haggai, Zechariah, and Malachi). The Manual of Discipline, the War scroll, the Thanksgiving Psalms, and a number of apocryphal and pseudepigraphal works (noncanonical, nonapocry-

37

phal Jewish documents written between 200 B.C. and A.D. 200) were also in the Qumran library suggesting, perhaps, that these Jews had not yet decided finally which writings deserved to be considered as sacred scripture.

What Was Found in Caves V-XI?

Cave V at Qumran was discovered by the archaeologists who were excavating Cave IV. Cave V was excavated September 22-24, 1952. It is located directly north of Cave IV, and like Cave IV is probably an artificial cave hollowed out of the marl cliffs by human hands. It may have served as a dwelling for one of the members of the ancient community of Qumran. Apart from a few pieces of phylacteries, fragments of the book of Tobias, and some biblical fragments, nothing of great value was found in Cave V. Almost all this material was in an advanced state of deterioration.

The Bedouins discovered Cave VI. One report says that they were offering this material for sale as early as September 13, 1952. The official excavators identified the cave on September 27. A peculiar feature of Cave VI is the fact that the fragments are predominantly papyrus rather than leather. Ordinarily, the sectarians preferred leather, but the scrolls of Cave VI proved to be the exception. Papyrus manuscripts of both Daniel and I and II Kings have been found here, along with some fragments of the Damascus Document.

This latter document, telling of a group of covenanters, has been well known since the turn of the century when Solomon Schechter published some fragments found in the genizah of a synagogue in Old Cairo. For many years, some scholars have felt that these so-called Zadokite Fragments (the elect described therein are considered to be the sons of Zadok) might be pre-Christian in origin. The finding of fragments in Caves IV and VI, which have a content remarkably similar to that known in the Cairo Damascus Document, leads many scholars to conclude that the Cairo fragments were really copied from, or at least patterned after, a pre-Christian Damascus Document which told about the life and beliefs of the Qumran sectarians.

Caves VII-X were found by the archaeologists during the fourth season of excavations at Khirbet Qumran. This means that these caves were found sometime between February 2 and April 6, 1955. While the contents of these caves are of considerable interest to specialists, they have little interest for the layman, and can be omitted in our present discussion.

The only cave at Qumran we have not yet discussed is Cave XI. It was discovered in either January or February of 1956. We are told that the completeness of the scrolls in this cave rivals that of the scrolls found in Caves I and IV. In addition to a well-preserved copy of Psalms (see chap. four), Cave XI has produced a very fine small scroll of part of Leviticus, some large pieces of an apocalypse of the New Jerusalem, and an Aramaic Targum (a translation or pharaphrase) of Job. Most of this material has not yet been dealt with in any detail either in the popular press or in scholarly journals, so we shall have to wait until the specialists have done their work on the contents of Cave XI.

What Did the Archaeologists Find in the Caves at Murabbaat?

The story of Murabbaat begins late in the year 1951, when fragments of unknown origin began to appear in Jerusalem. It soon became obvious that these fragments did not come from Qumran but from another unknown location. When the Bedouins came to Father de Vaux and attempted to sell some of these fragments to him, he suggested that their price was too high. They argued that the price was not too high because the caves from which these new Dead Sea Scrolls were coming were so nearly inaccessible that only perseverance and daring plus dusty and arduous labor on the part of the Bedouins could ever recover these new scrolls.

Father de Vaux thereupon suggested that he be permitted to accompany them and help them in their work. At first, the natives refused and explained that a stranger in the desert might attract the police and bring an end to their work. Father de Vaux, however, was quite equal to the task, and before the conversations had ended he had convinced the Bedouins to take him, the Director of Antiquities, a police escort, and an Arab foreman along with them to their new site.

It was January 21, 1952, when this band of men made its trek across the hills south and east of Bethlehem. Their destination was Murabbaat. As the officials neared the caves, they could see the natives scurrying for cover. A little more diplomacy convinced a number of the Bedouins to stay on as hired members of the expedition and soon the work was under way.

For six weeks, until March 3, the party explored four caves at Murabbaat and learned some most interesting things. For instance, they found an adz handle which was approximately six thousand years old, an age that was confirmed by a number of shards that belonged to the Chalcolithic period of three to four thousand years before the time of Christ. These caves, then, had had a long history of habitation. Indeed, flint tools were also unearthed. People had lived in these caves down through the ages, leaving evidence behind them for Harding and his crew to find. In the Chalcolithic period, the Middle Bronze Age (perhaps the sixteenth century before Christ), and the Iron Age (after 1200 B.C) people had lived in these caves for longer or shorter periods of time.

But so far as the story of the Dead Sea Scrolls is concerned, the most valuable finds in the Murabbaat area were the manuscripts and documents. These came from the second century A.D., many of them from the period of the second Jewish revolt (A.D. 132-35), and were invaluable because some of the letters were dated to this very period.

Now, the paleographer had a dated script with which to work as he tried to date the script of the Qumran manuscripts. Happily, there seemed little doubt that the script of Murabbaat was considerably later than that from Qumran. The evidence for an early dating of the Dead Sea Scrolls from Qumran was beginning to fall into place. First, there were the linen wrappers and pottery from the Roman period, and now dated documents from the second century A.D. with a script which was demonstrably later than that of the original Dead Sea Scrolls. When we add to all this evidence the fact that the excavations at Khirbet Qumran indicate this community was destroyed in A.D. 68, we can make a strong case for a pre–A.D. 68 date for all the Dead Sea Scrolls from Qumran, with the possible exception of the copper scrolls.

Greek, Hebrew, and Aramaic texts have come from Cave II at Murabbaat. There is, for instance, a Greek-language marriage contract which can be dated to A.D. 124. Even more important is a Hebrew papyrus letter of Simon ben Kosebah (the well-known Bar Kokheba who led the ill-fated second Jewish revolt) to a Joshua ben Galgola. It is just possible that Joshua ben Galgola was a commander of Bar Kokheba revolutionary forces at Murabbaat. At least the letter indicates that Hebrew was still used in correspondence in the second century A.D., and it shows us the correct spelling of Bar Kokheba's last name.

Late in 1954, the Beduoins brought in a Hebrew scroll of the minor prophets and offered it for sale at the Palestine Archaeological Museum. They wanted several thousand dollars for their latest discovery. It soon appeared that these Beduoins had discovered a fifth cave at Murabbaat. Their latest scroll was in an excellent state of preservation (at least in comparison with the other documents from Murabbaat). It was a second century A.D. scroll which included the latter half of Joel, Amos, Obadiah, Jonah, Micah, Nahum, Habakkuk, Zephaniah, and Haggai. It is interesting to note that this scroll, like all the other biblical fragments from Murabbaat, supports the traditional Hebrew text (the so-called Masoretic text) in its close agreement with it.

One other document deserves brief mention before we leave

the Murabbaat discoveries. It is a papyrus palimpsest (a piece of papyrus that has been erased and reused) containing a list of names and numbers. This document is noteworthy because it may be the oldest script we have from either Qumran or Murabbaat. Cross now dates both the superimposed script and the erased script in the seventh century B.C., though he notes that Milik, who is to publish the text, favors an eighth-century B.C. date. It is, in either case, the oldest papyrus inscribed in Hebrew ever to come out of Palestine.[2]

What Happened to the Original Dead Sea Scrolls from Cave I at Qumran?

The Hebrew University scrolls (War scroll, Isaiah scroll, and the Thanksgiving Psalms) stayed at the Hebrew University. The home they found in 1947 was to be a permanent one. The tourist who goes to Israel today may still see these scrolls on display every day of the week except Saturday. They are, in fact, a major tourist attraction.

Each morning at 8:30, a heavy vault door swings open in the basement of the Sherman building on the campus of the Hebrew University in Jerusalem and tourists stream into a small, windowless room to see Israel's collection of Dead Sea Scrolls. A woman who works there told me that from one to three thousand people come to see the scrolls each day.

The more exciting story concerns the fortunes of the St. Mark's scrolls which had been purchased by the Metropolitan Samuel. Both Burrows and Trever warned Samuel that it was dangerous to keep valuable scrolls in Jerusalem in 1948 when tension was high and actual warfare was an ever present possibility. It is not clear, however, that either Burrows or Trever recommended that the scrolls be taken out of Jordan, as some reports on the subject would seem to imply. On the contrary, it is obvious that both Burrows and Trever reminded Samuel

---

[2] Cf. F. M. Cross, *Ancient Library of Qumran*, p. 18.

about the antiquities laws of the country which forbade the removal of the scrolls from Jordan.

For one reason or another Samuel did not heed the advice of the Americans, but sent the scrolls out of the country, probably to Beirut. Harding does not mince words when he describes this action. He says that the archbishop (a metropolitan is similar to an archbishop) smuggled the scrolls out of the country. *Smuggle* is a strong word, but in this case it may be precise. Samuel did need an export license before taking the scrolls out of Jordan, but he never requested one. This questionable action on the part of Samuel may explain the hesitance of prospective buyers when Samuel finally offered "his" scrolls for sale.

Samuel himself left Jerusalem in the latter part of 1948. He went to Beirut, picked up the scrolls, and moved on to Egypt preparatory to sailing for the United States. In America, failing to find a buyer for his scrolls, Samuel finally resorted to an advertisement in the *Wall Street Journal* for June 1, 1954. Located among the "Miscellaneous for Sale" items in the classified directory, Samuel's ad ran as follows:

"The Four Dead Sea Scrolls"
Biblical Manuscripts dating back to at least
200 B.C. are for sale. This would be an ideal
gift to an educational or religious institution
by an individual or group.

Following the advertisement was an address, Box F 206, the *Wall Street Journal*. The scrolls were for sale on the open market to anyone who could and would pay the price.

By coincidence, Yigael Yadin was at that very moment in the United States lecturing on the scrolls. Yadin, the son of the late Sukenik, soon learned about this advertisement and determined to buy these manuscripts for the state of Israel if they were actually the original Dead Sea Scrolls.

Yadin's account of the subsequent negotiations has the flavor of a detective story in which the investigator is about to "zero in" on the object of a long search.[3] In order not to reveal his own identity and thereby give away the secret that he wanted to purchase the scrolls for the state of Israel, Yadin arranged for an intermediary to meet with Samuel's representative, Charles Manoog. It immediately became apparent that the scrolls could not be bought cheaply. Samuel was asking $250,000. Would the prospective buyer be willing to pay such an amount? Yadin's representative assured Manoog that his client would consider such a figure if these were the same Dead Sea Scrolls which had been found in 1947 by Muhammad adh-Dhib.

In due course Manoog produced the scrolls and Yadin, in turn, arranged to have the authenticity of the manuscripts verified by a competent biblical scholar. Convinced that these were the same scrolls his own father had tried to purchase from Anton Kiraz in 1948, Yadin agreed to buy the scrolls. Sukenik had died on February 28, 1953, but his ambition to acquire the scrolls for Israel was about to be realized through his own son, Yadin.

Samuel Gottesman, a wealthy industrialist of New York City, generously agreed to help buy the scrolls for Israel. According to Mr. Cherrick, who is the Executive Vice-Chairman of the Board of Governors of the Hebrew University, Gottesman donated $150,000 toward the purchase price. The American Fund for Israeli Institutions offered another hundred thousand dollars, and soon the scrolls were on their way to their new home in Israel.

Today, as the result of the benefactions of the Gottesman Foundation, a special sanctuary for the scrolls is being constructed in Jerusalem. It will be called "The Shrine of the Book" and will be located on a five-acre tract of land near the Hebrew University and the Knesset building. Having just returned from Jerusalem, I know that the building is not yet finished; but if the work progresses according to schedule, the

[3] Cf. Yigael Yadin, *The Message of the Scrolls,* pp. 39-52, for an absorbing account of this entire transaction.

Gottesman scrolls (so-called since March of 1955) will be moved from their vault in the Sherman building to their own sanctuary in 1963. Most of this structure, with the exception of the dome, will be below ground level. It is thought that this rather unusual architectural design will serve as a reminder that the scrolls originally came from a cave.[4]

What Happened to the Scrolls Which Remained in Jordan?

As we have already seen, the Bedouins brought in their fragments by the thousands and sold them to the Palestine Archaeological Museum. Inside this museum there was a room called a "scrollery" where these fragments were collected, cleaned, sorted, put together like a jigsaw puzzle, photographed, and finally published for the benefit of the scholarly world.

An international team of scholars representing both the Catholic and the Protestant faiths co-operated in an attempt to unravel the mysteries of these scrolls as soon as possible. From America, there was Frank Cross of Harvard and Monsignor Patrick Skehan of the Catholic University of America. England was represented by John Allegro of Manchester University and John Strugnell of Oxford. Fathers Barthélemy and Starcky came from France. Claus-Hunno Huntzinger of Göttingen contributed German to the babel of languages in the "scrollery," and Father Milik of Poland was the final member of the panel of experts.

These men had one thing in common. They were disciplined scholars dedicated to the search for truth. Nationalities and religious orientations became secondary as they made a team effort to translate the texts which lay before them.

Occasionally, the workers would engage in friendly competition to see who could decipher a given text first. Cross tells a story about such a contest of wits entered into by Allegro, Milik, and himself, a story which has a humorous twist to it. The three

[4] *New York Times,* December 18, 1961.

scholars agreed to compete to see which of them would be first to break a mysterious code that appeared on one of the scroll fragments. The unwritten rules for the competition seemed to be that each man would start and end his effort at the same time, so that no one would have an unfair advantage. Lunch time came while the young savants were still puzzling over their problem. Allegro and Cross returned early from their lunch and fell into a discussion of the ethics of continuing their race before Father Milik returned. "Of course," says Cross, "[we] proceeded without him." A few minutes later, Milik came triumphantly into the scrollery announcing that he had cracked the code during the lunch hour aided by photographs of the fragments which he had taken with him! [5]

Most of the preliminary work of cleaning and sorting the scrolls has now been done. The international team no longer meets in Jerusalem. The official publication of these Jordanian scrolls is still in process, but the world is already indebted to the students of the scrolls who have given their time and their effort to restore these ancient manuscripts.

[5] Cross, *Ancient Library of Qumran,* p. 45.

III

Treasures from Caves
An Introduction to Some of the Dead Sea Scrolls

What Has Happened to the So-called Lamech Scroll?

THE GELATINIZED CONDITION OF THE LAMECH SCROLL, ONE OF the original scrolls from Cave I, made it obvious from the beginning that great care would have to be exercised if this scroll were ever to reveal its secrets. The decaying leather was so dry and brittle that rough handling was almost certain to cause crumbling and disintegration. It was this state of deterioration that prompted Millar Burrows to say, "only very careful, expert treatment can ever unroll enough to recover any considerable part of the text, if indeed this is possible at all." [1]

Nevertheless, it is quite likely that American specialists could have performed the delicate operation of unrolling the Lamech scroll had the Metropolitan Samuel been willing to part with it. John Coolidge, director of the Fogg Art Museum, estimated that the job of unrolling the scroll might take about six months. Chemical treatment would be necessary, but the scroll could be unrolled.[2] Samuel, however, preferred to hold on to the scroll until a buyer had been found for all the scrolls he had in his

[1] Millar Burrows, *The Dead Sea Scrolls* (New York: The Viking Press, 1955), pp. 26-27.
[2] *New York Times*, January 14, 1950.

possession. It was for this reason that the task of unrolling the Lamech scroll fell into the hands of the Israeli scholars.

In 1954, Yigael Yadin arranged to buy the scrolls from Samuel, and soon Israel received her newly purchased treasures. James Bieberkraut, a very talented Jewish scholar who had had much experience restoring ancient documents in Munich, was entrusted with the responsibility of opening the Lamech scroll. Assisted by two Jewish professors from the Hebrew University in Jerusalem, Yadin and Avigad, Bieberkraut began the humidification process which would eventually make the leather of the scroll sufficiently pliable for unrolling. The relative humidity was kept around 75 per cent and the temperature at approximately sixty-three degrees Fahrenheit. After two weeks of this treatment it began to appear that the nineteen hundred-year-old scroll, which had been in modern hands since 1947, would at last yield its secrets to the gentle prying of Bieberkraut.

The formal announcement that Lamech had been opened came on February 7, 1956. Benjamin Mazar, president of the Hebrew University, made the announcement. The actual separating of the leather leaves had taken fifteen months, during which period it had been necessary to rehumidify the document in order to keep it from crumbling. But at last, nine years after the scroll had been discovered, and aided by infrared photography, much of the long-hidden script could be read.

On the basis of these early readings it was decided that it would be inappropriate to continue referring to this document as the Lamech scroll. It did indeed tell about Lamech, son of Methuselah and father of Noah, but it contained much more. There were stories about Noah and his birth as well as tales about Abraham and Sarah, his wife. Perhaps the "Scroll of the Patriarchs," or "A Genesis Apocryphon" would be a more appropriate title. At least this was the thinking of the Israeli scholars; and, following their lead, it has become common practice among scholars to refer to this scroll by one or the other of these latter titles.

What Are the Contents of the Genesis Apocryphon?

The official publication of the entire scroll has not yet been made, but thanks to Yadin and Avigad, Dead Sea Scrolls enthusiasts have not had to wait for the final publication in order to be introduced to the contents of the Genesis Apocryphon. In *A Genesis Apocryphon,* published in Jerusalem by the Magnes Press in 1956, Avigad and Yadin made available in English translation a colorful description of Sarah which appears in this scroll. After describing the beauty of Sarah's face, the scroll continues as follows:

And how . . . fine is the hair of her head, how fair indeed are her eyes and how pleasing her nose and all the radiance of her face . . . how beautiful her breast and how lovely all her whiteness. Her arms goodly to look upon, and her hands how perfect . . . all the appearance of her hands. How fair her palms and how long and fine all the fingers of her hands. Her legs how beautiful and how without blemish her thighs. And all maidens and all brides that go beneath the wedding canopy are not more fair than she. And above all women she is lovely and higher is her beauty than that of them all, and with all her beauty there is much wisdom in her.[3]

For a proper appreciation of this description of Sarah, we must remember the biblical passages to which it makes reference. In the twelfth chapter of Genesis we read of Abraham's and Sarah's approach to Egypt. Abraham fears for his life because Sarah is so beautiful that the Pharaoh will surely desire her and may even kill Abraham to get her. Abraham urges Sarah to say that she is his sister so that all may go well with him. Happily, the Lord protects Sarah when she is taken into the Pharaoh's house, and her virtue is not compromised.

The second column of the Genesis Apocryphon contains the end of an equally interesting story about the birth of Lamech's

[3] Nahman Avigad and Yigael Yadin, *A Genesis Apocryphon* (Jerusalem: The Magnes Press of the Hebrew University and Heikhal Ha-Sefer, 1956), p. 43. The English translation was actually prepared by Mrs. Schulamith Schwartz Nardi.

49

son, undoubtedly Noah, though the actual name is not given in the scroll. It is unfortunate that so few words remain in the first column of the Genesis Apocryphon that it can only be conjectured how the story began; but beginning at the top of column two it is seen that Lamech is troubled by the birth of this child. Apparently the baby is so unusual that Lamech questions his own paternity. (There is a story in the pseudepigraphal book of Enoch which tells how the baby Noah, while still in the hands of the midwife, began to converse with the Lord of Righteousness. Some scholars conclude that this is the part of the story which was originally included in the first column of the Genesis Apocryphon.)

Lamech thinks that his wife, Bat Enosh, may have consorted with the angels (literally, the wakeful ones) and that this fact explains the strange behavior of the newborn son. Bat Enosh, however, insists that the heavenly beings have had nothing to do with this conception. Indeed, the accusation of Lamech seems so unfair to her that she controls her indignation with difficulty and says to Lamech, "I swear to thee by the great Holy One . . . that thine is this seed and from thee is this conception and from thee was the fruit formed." [4] When Bat Enosh denies that the angels have had anything to do with her conception, Lamech goes to his father, Methuselah, for advice. Methuselah in turn goes to *his* father, Enoch. Unfortunately, the column ends here and we may never know just how the story ended. But it can be seen that once more the Genesis Apocryphon reflects material found in chapters five and six of the biblical book of Genesis.

Have the Copper Scrolls Been Unrolled?

Strictly speaking, it would be incorrect to say the copper scrolls have been unrolled. We can say, however, that these two scrolls have been sawed into strips.

[4] *Ibid.,* p. 40.

The two copper scrolls (consisting of three sheets of metal, and originally one scroll) were found on March 20, 1952, and for three years after the scrolls had been removed from Cave III to the Palestine Archaeological Museum in Jerusalem, scholars wondered if these thoroughly oxidized sheets could ever be unwrapped without serious damage to the script.

Alsoph H. Corwin of the Johns Hopkins University in Baltimore, Maryland, examined a square centimeter of the material which had been brought to him and began to experiment in an attempt to devise a method for restoring the original metal, a method which would not damage the writing engraved thereon. Corwin was having some success with his work but, as in the case of the Genesis Apocryphon, time ran out before he had perfected his method. It was in 1955 that John Allegro of the University of Manchester recommended that the scrolls be brought from Jordan to Manchester, England, for opening. G. Lankester Harding of the Jordanian Department of Antiquities requested, and obtained, permission from the government to take one of the copper scrolls out of the country. By July 13, 1955, the smaller of the two scrolls had arrived at the Manchester College of Technology where H. Wright Baker of the department of mechanical engineering had agreed to study the scroll and make suggestions for opening it.[5]

It did not take the ingenious Baker long to devise a plan. What might be described as a miniature flatcar was equipped with a vertical post at each end which would support the scroll once spindles had been inserted in it. The car itself could be moved along rails by a slight twist of a knob attached to the left front wheel.

The copper scroll was prepared for its forthcoming "surgery" by the application of a tough, low-shrinkage plastic which was baked and cured in an electric oven at the very moderate tem-

[5] Cf. J. M. Allegro, *The Dead Sea Scrolls,* pp. 181 ff.

51

perature of 104 degrees Fahrenheit. Aluminum spindles were inserted in each end of the scroll and held in place by dental plaster. The scroll was mounted on the flatcar so that the longitudinal axis of the scroll was parallel to the longitudinal axis of the flatcar.

One other item was essential—a saw. A circular saw approximately one-and-three-quarter inches in diameter was spring-loaded and mounted above the scroll so that a gentle pressure from the operator's finger would depress the saw and bring it into contact with the metal. Since this particular saw would not make a cut wider than six thousandths of an inch, there was a good possibility that a skilled technician could saw between the very strokes the original scribe had made without destroying any letters.

Baker proved to be a master technician. So skillfully did he do his work that not a single letter was destroyed by the process of sawing. Baker took care to avoid cuts along scribal lines that ran parallel with the cut of the saw, cutting only across diagonal or horizontal strokes. He had begun his sawing on September 30, 1955. He completed it on January 16, 1956. The scrolls which Baker described as "literally clasping their secrets to their hearts" were now ready for transcription and translation.[6]

Does the Copper Document Tell of Hidden Treasures?

As early as 1953 a German scholar, K. G. Kuhn, visited the Palestine Archaeological Museum and peered intently at the copper scrolls which had not yet been unrolled. With the patience of a sleuth determined to unravel a mystery, Kuhn studied the Hebrew letters which appeared in reverse, or in negative, on the back side of the copper sheets. It is a credit to Kuhn that, on the basis of this preliminary investigation, he guessed correctly that the scrolls, when unrolled, would prove to be a list of hidden treasures.

[6] H. W. Baker, "How the Dead Sea Scrolls Were Opened," *Engineering*, Vol. 181, Part 2, 1956, pp. 194-96.

The fact is that the copper document lists at least sixty hiding places (one report says sixty-four) for gold and silver. These places may be located as far north as Gerizim and as far south as Hebron, a distance of about fifty miles, but the majority of the treasures seem to be buried in the Jerusalem area. Tombs, watchtowers, fortresses, cisterns, and underground passages are favorite hiding places. Unfortunately these sites are not pinpointed precisely, so it will be exceedingly difficult to use the copper document as an easy guide to sudden wealth.

But are we dealing here with actual treasures? Is the copper document the work of a crank? Is this folklore, or do we have here the description of the wealth of the Qumran community? Maybe these frugal, hard-working people who lived near the northwestern tip of the Dead Sea really did amass a small fortune which they hid for safekeeping. Or perhaps we have here a description of the treasures of the temple. If so, which temple?

Scholars are divided in their opinions about the correct answers to these questions. A British expedition led by Allegro set out on April 13, 1960, to look for more scrolls and for some of the gold and silver mentioned in the copper document. By April 19, Allegro was digging for buried treasure inside the Old City of Jerusalem.[7] Thus far, these attempts have been futile.

Perhaps Milik, who was the member of the international scroll team officially responsible for the deciphering and publication of the copper document, is correct when he says, "It goes almost without saying that the document is not an historical record of actual treasures buried in antiquity." [8] Those who reject the theory that we are dealing with actual treasures argue that it is unlikely that either the people of Qumran or even the temple of Herod possessed such great wealth. According to the copper document, more than 4,500 talents of gold and silver were hidden away. If we consider the common talent of the Old Testament period to be equal to approximately

[7] *New York Times,* April 14, 1960. Cf. *Jerusalem Post,* April 13, 1960.

[8] J. T. Milik, "The Copper Document from Cave III, Qumran," *Biblical Archaeologist* XIX (1956), 63.

seventy-five pounds, and assume that our scribe had this talent in mind, the amount of hidden treasure would exceed 170 tons. If the scribe had Ezekiel's eighty-eight pound talent in mind there would be more than two hundred tons. Allegro, in an attempt to keep the amount of treasure within a reasonable limit, suggests that when the scribe mentions the talent he really has in mind the twelve-ounce mina. Allegro points out that if this hypothesis is accepted, a jar which, according to the copper document, holds eighty talents would in reality contain about sixty pounds.[9]

Another objection to the view that the copper document lists real treasure is that the scroll is inscribed with imperfect skill by a clumsy scribe who uses a colloquial dialect and supplies only vague information about the precise location of the hiding places. And is a burial depth of thirteen-and-one-half feet likely? These and similar questions plague those who would know the truth about this matter.

Those who are inclined to believe that the copper document does list actual treasure point out that the very use of costly copper is evidence that a real treasure is being described. Moreover, in the final column of the copper document another copy of this document is mentioned. Add to this the possibility that the Jewish Zealots who controlled the Jerusalem temple for a short time prior to its destruction by the Romans in A.D. 70 may have prepared the copper document as a reminder of where they had hidden the wealth of the Temple, and it is obvious why caution is advisable in drawing final conclusions about the copper scrolls.

What Is the Habakkuk Commentary?

The Habakkuk Commentary, one of the original Dead Sea Scrolls from Cave I, is an explanation and interpretation of the verses of scripture which appear in chapters one and two of the

[9] J. M. Allegro, *The Treasure of the Copper Scroll* (Garden City, N. Y.: Doubleday & Co., Inc., 1960) , p. 135, n. 8.

biblical book of Habakkuk. It is noteworthy that the Habakkuk Commentary does not include an interpretation of the third chapter of the biblical book of Habakkuk. Even prior to the discovery of the Dead Sea Scrolls many writers had suggested that the third chapter of Habakkuk had been added to the work of the prophet at a later time. This theory now receives new support.

Before answering the question about the Habakkuk Commentary in more detail, it may be helpful to say a few words about the biblical book of Habakkuk. In its present form there seems to be a reference to the Babylonians (the Chaldeans of vs. 6), whose mighty armies have just defeated the Egyptians in the Battle of Carchemish (605 B.C.). As the prophet considers this "bitter and hasty nation, who march through the breadth of the earth, to seize habitations not their own" (Hab. 1:6), and remembers Judah's unhappy experiences with Assyrian domination, he questions whether justice really does prevail upon the earth. Theory suggests that the righteous should prosper, but the facts indicate that violence, destruction, and wickedness prevail in the late seventh century when the prophet speaks. Under such circumstances, what can one do but take his stand upon the watchtower and trust that the "righteous shall live by his faith" (Hab. 2:4b)?

With this content in mind, we turn now to see how the Habakkuk Commentary from Qumran interprets our biblical book. According to modern standards of biblical exegesis, we would expect to find some reference to the Babylonians and to seventh-century history, but such is not the case. After citing part of the biblical text of Hab. 1:6 (and here it should be noted that the Habakkuk Commentary has great value because it provides a textual witness to scripture which is about one thousand years older than the one commonly used prior to the finding of the Dead Sea Scrolls), the Qumran author informs us that this verse really refers to the Kittim (or Kitti'im), who are probably the Romans of his own time. What he does, therefore, is to apply Habakkuk's prophecy to his own situation, thereby making the older prophetic pronouncement contemporary with his own position in history, a practice not unknown among biblical interpreters of the twentieth century.

Why Has the Habakkuk Commentary Aroused So Much Controversy?

Relatively early in the era of the scrolls, André Dupont-Sommer of the Sorbonne in Paris, studied the Habakkuk Commentary and on the basis of one of the passages concluded that the sect's leader, the well-known Teacher of Righteousness, was regarded by his followers as having had a pre-existent life prior to his becoming flesh. The passage in question comes in the commentary on Hab. 2:7, where there is a reference to someone suffering "in his body of flesh." In his first study of this passage, Dupont-Sommer was of the opinion that the suffering was that of the Teacher of Righteousness, and he accordingly said, "without doubt he was a divine being who 'became flesh' to live and die as a man." [10] Other passages in this same Habakkuk Commentary convinced Dupont-Sommer that the members of the sect thought of their leader as a divine master who became flesh, suffered, died, and lived again to return in glory at the end of the age.

These conjectures on the part of Dupont-Sommer aroused interest and stirred controversy as soon as they came to the attention of the scholarly world. The experts who had been working with the Habakkuk Commentary were quick to point out that the phrase "in his body of flesh" does not necessarily imply either incarnation or pre-existence. It may simply refer to the normal life of the individual without any overtones. Even more crucial is the fact that the Hebrew text of the Habakkuk Commentary is so incomplete that it is not easy to deter-

[10] André Dupont-Sommer, *The Dead Sea Scrolls*, trans. E. Margaret Rowley (New York: The Macmillan Company, 1952), p. 34. Used by permission of The Macmillan Company and Basil Blackwell.

mine just who it is that suffers "in his body of flesh." It is at least equally possible that the archenemy of the Teacher of Righteousness, the Wicked Priest, is the subject of this sentence. Interestingly enough, even Dupont-Sommer has now abandoned his earlier interpretation that pre-existence and incarnation are suggested by the phrase "in his body of flesh."

Unfortunately, there is another passage in the Habakkuk Commentary which is even more difficult to translate and understand. In the commentary on Hab. 2:15 there are four lines of scroll text which can be translated as follows:

Its interpretation concerns the Wicked Priest who pursued after the Teacher of Righteousness in order to swallow him up in the anger of his wrath, in the house of his exile; and at the time of the festival of rest, the Day of Atonement, he appeared to them to swallow them up and make them stumble on the day of fasting, their sabbath rest.

If the reader regards this as an ambiguous translation, at least one purpose will have been served. The very difficulty of making sense out of this passage should warn the layman to be somewhat skeptical when writers on the subject of the Habakkuk Commentary assure him that there is a passage therein which indicates that the author of the Habakkuk Commentary describes both the death and the subsequent reappearance of the Teacher of Righteousness.

It is true that this passage could be translated to read, "the Wicked Priest persecuted the Teacher of Righteousness in order to destroy him," and hence it might be concluded that the Wicked Priest succeeded in killing the Teacher of Righteousness. But—and this must be stressed—both this translation and the inference drawn from it are highly tenuous.

Dupont-Sommer points out that the word translated as "appeared" is often used to describe the appearance of Yahweh (the divine name in the Old Testament) and hence is probabl·

used in the Habakkuk Commentary to describe the supernatural reappearance of the Teacher of Righteousness. Two
objections can be raised against this hypothesis. First, there
is no certainty that the Hebrew verb must always suggest a
divine manifestation or revelation of supernatural glory. Just as
the "ghost" of the seventeenth century became the "spirit" of
the twentieth century, so Hebrew words underwent an evolution in meaning which calls for caution when translating late
Hebrew texts.

The second objection to Dupont-Sommer's interpretation
concerns the subject of the verb "appeared." Is the Wicked
Priest or the Teacher of Righteousness the one who appeared?
According to the meaning and translation of this text, it is the
Wicked Priest. If this assumption is correct, there would be no
reason to argue that the verb "appeared" has supernatural con-
notations in the present text.

The reader may be surprised to learn that such an ambiguous
text has caused so much controversy, but it is precisely such
ambiguity which causes difficulty. These are the texts over
which even the best-trained scholars (and Dupont-Sommer is
certainly one of them) can find themselves in honest disagree-
ment.

Have Other Commentaries Been Found in the Caves?

Fragmentary evidence of a number of commentaries has been
found in the caves near the ruins of Qumran. Cave I has
produced, in addition to the Habakkuk Commentary discussed
above, fragments of commentaries on Psalms, Micah, and
Zephaniah. And from Cave IV comes evidence of more commentaries on Psalms, Isaiah, and Nahum. There seems to be
little doubt that the Jews who lived at Qumran spent much
time studying, interpreting, and copying scripture.

We cannot discuss each of these commentaries in detail, nor
is it necessary to do so for the purposes of the present work, but
attention should be given to one of these commentaries which

has caused considerable discussion in the popular press. I refer, of course, to the Nahum Commentary, which was found in Cave IV.

The controversy over this particular commentary began early in 1956 when John Allegro announced in a BBC broadcast (January 23, 1956) that he had found new evidence that the Teacher of Righteousness had been crucified.[11] When the news of Allegro's latest claim came to the attention of the public, excitement was aroused. Interested lay people remembered that the uniqueness of Jesus had seemingly been questioned by other writers, and they began to wonder if there really were a religious leader who had lived in Palestine just before the time of Jesus and had been crucified as Jesus was. Perhaps Dupont-Sommer had been correct when he suggested that the Galilean Master was in many respects "an astonishing reincarnation of the Master of Justice." [12]

The details of Allegro's conjecture are too complex to be of interest to the average lay reader, so perhaps it will suffice to say that the eminent British Semitist, H. H. Rowley of Manchester University, prepared a written evaluation of Allegro's hypothesis and had it published in the September, 1956, issue of the *Journal of Biblical Literature*.[13] In this article, Rowley pointed out that there is absolutely no clear evidence in the Nahum Commentary that the Teacher of Righteousness was crucified. Having presented his own evidence in the clear and forceful manner that is characteristic of him, Rowley concluded that Allegro may have started with a preconception and

[11] Cf. *Time*, February 6, 1956, and Millar Burrows, *More Light on the Dead Sea Scrolls* (New York: The Viking Press, 1958), p. 217.

[12] A. Dupont-Sommer, *The Dead Sea Scrolls*, p. 99. Miss Rowley translates "Master of Justice" instead of the more common "Teacher of Righteousness." Cf. A. Dupont-Sommer, *The Jewish Sect of Qumran and the Essenes*, p. 160, where Dupont-Sommer says that he merely intended to "stimulate the curiosity of the reader, without pretending to solve a most complex problem at the price of oversimplification."

[13] H. H. Rowley, "4QpNahum and the Teacher of Righteousness," *Journal of Biblical Literature* LXXV (1956), 188-93.

then filled in the text of the Nahum Commentary so it would agree with his theory. Rowley goes on to say that this "savors more of propaganda for a theory than of objective scholarship." Since 1956, a majority of scholars have agreed with Rowley that there is no unambiguous evidence in the Nahum Commentary for Allegro's theory that the Teacher of Righteousness was crucified.

IV

More Treasures from Caves

*Are the Thanksgiving Psalms Similar to the Psalms
and Poetry of the Old Testament?*

THE THANKSGIVING PSALMS BELONG TO THAT PORTION OF THE
Dead Sea Scrolls acquired by Sukenik in December of 1947.
Had we had the good fortune to see these psalms when they
were first purchased, it is doubtful whether we would have believed that a few years later a critical student of the scrolls
would say that this scroll was without doubt the jewel of the
mystical literature from Qumran and one of the most valuable
scrolls of the sect.[1] When Sukenik first saw the matted bundles
of this scroll, with three sheets crumpled together in one section
and about seventy fragments packed tightly together in a second
mass, he felt that it had probably come from a genizah. While
this view is still accepted by several scholars, we now know that
a high degree of literary artistry is to be seen in the forty
(twenty more or less complete and about twenty represented in
fragmentary form) hymns of the Thanksgiving Psalms.

Consider these words of the poet:

> I thank thee, O Lord,
> because thou hast put my soul in the bundle of life;

[1] A. Dupont-Sommer, *Die Essenischen Schriften Vom Toten Meer* trans. Walter W. Müller (Tübingen: J. C. B. Mohr [Paul Siebeck], 1960), p. 217.

thou hast fenced me off from all the snares of the pit.
Oppressors sought my life,
while I laid hold on thy covenant.
But they are a worthless company,
a congregation of Belial.
They do not know that thou hast made me stand,
and in thy steadfast love thou wilt save my life,
for from thee are my steps.[2]

Nor is this an isolated example of the poet's devotion. In at least a dozen of these hymns the writer begins by saying, "I thank thee, O Lord," and then goes on to express his deep gratitude for knowledge, for the power to praise God even though he is a thing of clay, for strength to stand in the presence of the unrighteous, and for the abundant mercy of God which pardons the guilty one. It is the prevalent mood of thanksgiving expressed verbally in these hymns which prompted Sukenik to call this the Thanksgiving scroll.

Since subjective preferences may enter into any evaluation of poems and their relationship to other hymns, it is wise not to be dogmatic, but I cannot refrain from saying that in my own opinion it is extremely difficult to improve upon some of the biblical psalms. Perhaps long acquaintance increases appreciation, but when the psalmist of the Old Testament sings out,

Whither shall I go from thy Spirit?
Or whither shall I flee from thy presence?
If I ascend to heaven, thou art there!
If I make my bed in Sheol, thou art there!
If I take the wings of the morning
and dwell in the uttermost parts of the sea,
even there thy hand shall lead me,
and thy right hand shall hold me.

—Ps. 139:7-10

we are touched by an inspiration which is neither surpassed nor matched in the Thanksgiving Psalms.

Nor can the theology of suffering which we find in the Thanksgiving Psalms equal that of the unknown poet (we call him Second Isaiah for lack of a better name) who affirms the redemptive value of suffering as he writes,

> But he was wounded for our transgressions,
>   he was bruised for our iniquities;
> upon him was the chastisement that made us whole,
>   and with his stripes we are healed.
> All we like sheep have gone astray;
>   we have turned every one to his own way;
> and the Lord has laid on him
>   the iniquity of us all.
>
> —Isa. 53:5, 6

Other questions about this scroll, which need not detain us long in this study, are these: Did the Teacher of Righteousness compose these psalms? What do these psalms tell us about the date of the biblical psalms? To the latter question we answer simply that the style of the Thanksgiving Psalms is more like that of the Magnificat of Mary and the Benedictus of Zechariah than of the canonical psalms. This fact, plus the discovery of the Psalms scroll in Cave XI, will surely cause students of the canonical psalms to rethink the late date of authorship (as late as the first century B.C.) assigned to some of these psalms prior to the discovery of the Dead Sea Scrolls.

The answer to the first question is not so easy. We know that the Teacher of Righteousness suffered, and we can tell from reading the Thanksgiving Psalms that their author or authors also knew troubled days. They knew what it meant to be the subject (s) of derision and the storm center for the opposition. Still, there is no explicit textual evidence for considering the Teacher of Righteousness the author of any of these psalms. If one psalm speaks of the author's having been driven forth

63

from "my land" we may have evidence that the Teacher was the author, but this is not certain. My own conclusion is that the Teacher's authorship of at least some of the Thanksgiving Psalms is an attractive possibility but not a proven fact.

Do the Isaiah Scrolls Indicate That the Traditional Hebrew Text Is Accurate?

One evening, shortly after I had arrived home from doing an educational television program on the Dead Sea Scrolls, the telephone rang. When I answered, a troubled voice on the other end of the line asked, "Where is that verse of scripture in Isaiah which you said had been corrected in the Revised Standard Version in conformity with a reading in the Dead Sea Scroll of Isaiah?" When I replied that the example I had cited came from Isa. 33:8, the receiver clicked on the other end of the line and the conversation ended.

This seemingly trivial incident troubled me at the time because I had not intended to leave the impression that the traditional Hebrew text used prior to the discovery of the Dead Sea Scrolls (a text usually referred to as the Masoretic text, or simply MT by specialists) was unreliable. On the contrary, I wanted to leave the opposite impression, that the finding of the Dead Sea Scrolls tended to reassure us and confirm the general accuracy of the traditional Hebrew text. To be sure, the Isaiah scrolls from the Qumran caves do not always and in every small detail agree with the Masoretic text, but the variations are—certainly from a layman's point of view—minor, if not insignificant.

What some (and I hope that the number is small) of our lay people do not know is that we do not today have just one Hebrew text from which to work when we produce English translations of the Old Testament. We have many Hebrew texts representing variant readings, and often it is only a voice vote, the majority winning, which determines the Hebrew text to be used for the English translation. When this fact is properly recognized, as it should be, lay people will be able to appreciate more the value of an ancient scroll such as the Isaiah scroll (1QIs*), acquired by Athanasius Samuel in 1947.

Let us return for a moment to the example cited above, Isa. 33:8. In this particular verse the King James Version mentions "cities," whereas the Revised Standard Version reads "witnesses." In the Hebrew language, the difference between these two words is only a matter of one letter. If there is an *r* in the Hebrew word, it is "cities." If there is a *d* instead of an *r,* the word becomes "witnesses." The fact is that the Hebrew letters for *r* and *d* look so much alike they can easily be confused, especially if the material on which they are written is ancient and worn.

Textual critics had wondered about this particular verse long before anyone had ever heard of the Dead Sea Scrolls. Knowing that a *d* and an *r* could easily be confused in the Hebrew text, some of these critics had already suggested that the Masoretic text be emended to read "witnesses" rather than "cities," which had never made much sense. The finding of the large Isaiah scroll simply added new support to an old conjecture, and the English text was revised accordingly.

There is one other question which is almost always asked. Do the Isaiah scrolls from Qumran give any support to the view that there are really two, if not three, Isaiahs? Many interpreters of the biblical book of Isaiah, noting what they think to be a change of mood, writing style, and historical setting in the fortieth chapter, suggest that the author who produced this and the following chapters was not the same Isaiah who prophesied in the eighth century B.C. Accordingly, these scholars designate chs. 40 through 55 of our present book of Isaiah as Second Isaiah and, by similar reasoning, find a Third Isaiah in chs. 56 through 66.

That there are two, or even three, Isaiahs is more difficult for the lay mind to grasp than that different Bibles may represent variations in text. The layman, especially if he has a more traditional orientation in his view of the Bible, wonders if the finding of multiple Isaiahs may not be dependent upon the whim and theological predispositions of the higher critics. For this reason, he asks if the Dead Sea Scrolls confirm the theory of two or three Isaiahs.

The answer is that the Dead Sea Scrolls neither confirm nor disprove the theory of a multiple authorship for the book of Isaiah. On the one hand there is no break in the text of 1QIs^a (the large scroll that went to St. Mark's Monastery) after the thirty-ninth chapter. On the other hand, this does not prove much because it has long been assumed that this prophetic book was canonized (accepted as scripture) as early as 200 B.C., which would be about a century earlier than the copying of this particular scroll. Even if there were a Second Isaiah, it would have been a part of the scroll one hundred years before our scribe did his work.

What Is the War Scroll?

The War scroll (1QM is the technical designation in official publications; the M represents the first letter of the Hebrew word for "war") from Cave I is more properly called "The War of the Sons of Light with the Sons of Darkness." It is a detailed description of the final conflict between the members of the sect (the sons of light) and their enemies (the sons of darkness).

The Jews who first composed this scroll were convinced that they were living in the last days. God's wrath and vengeance were about to be visited upon the forces of darkness and error. The sons of light would have to rally and organize for the conflict and the struggle. The day of God's salvation was at hand. Vindication for God's elect would soon be realized. The angels of God would join in the war and fight on the side of the sons of light. With such divine assistance, the final outcome of the war was never in doubt.

The war would last for a period of forty years but there would only be thirty-five years of actual conflict because the elect did not intend to fight during sabbatical years. Fortunately, the enemies would also observe the sabbatical years (in deference to the sensibilities of their opponents?) and the elect would not be at any disadvantage because of their religious convictions!

There would be three major battles in this war. In the first two battles, lasting for six years, the sons of light would fight against such neighbors as Edom, Moab, Ammon, and Philistia. One of the battles would be against their own brethren who had violated the terms of the covenant. And if Yadin is correct—as I think he is—the sons of light would also fight against the Romans in Syria and in Egypt during this six-year period.

It was the third battle, however, which was to be the longest in duration and most severe. This campaign was to continue for twenty-nine years. For nine years the opponents would be the sons of Shem, such as the Mesopotamians, the Lydians, the Syrians, and those who were across the Euphrates. For the next ten years, the sons of light would wage War against the sons of Ham. In the final ten years, it is probable (the text is incomplete and the reconstruction is conjectural) that the sons of light would fight against the sons of Japheth. It may be that the author had in mind the sons of Japheth, Ham, and Shem, as they are listed in the tenth chapter of Genesis.

Both infantry and cavalry would participate in the war. There would be 28,000 infantrymen divided between the light and the heavy infantry. Men between the ages of forty and fifty could serve in the heavy infantry. There would be 21,000 of these. The prescribed age for membership in the light infantry was thirty to forty-five years. Seven thousand men would serve in these ranks. In similar fashion, the cavalry would be divided into light and heavy units with ages for riders corresponding to those prevailing in the infantry.

Horses and war matériel are described in detail. The horses were to be fleet stallions, full grown and experienced so they would not shy from odd sounds. They had to have excellent wind and tender mouths in order to respond quickly and easily to the riders' commands. The dimensions for the shields and the spears are given. Slogans are worked out and the use of trumpets is explained. In fact, so many instruments of war are described in this scroll that translators are not always certain just what the original author had in mind; but Yadin, who has had experience as a general in the Israeli army, thinks that the writer was influenced by knowledge of Roman arms and tactics.

Women, children, the blind, and the lame were to be excluded from the camp from the time the army moved out to war. Holy angels were to accompany the army, so all possible sources of contamination and ritual impurity had to be eliminated. Priests dressed in white robes and wearing linen trousers would play an active and important part in the war. They would sound the trumpets made from rams' horns to signal both the charge and the recall, albeit from a safe distance so they would not be defiled by contact with the impure blood of the enemy.

In the final battle, God would give victory to the sons of light. The God who led Israel out of Egypt would once more reveal his power, and the enemies would be utterly exterminated. No prisoners of war were to be taken. The God who enabled David to smite the mighty Goliath would once more fight for his people and for right. The day of reckoning was at hand.

Which Is the Oldest Hebrew Manuscript from Qumran?

There is an archaic Samuel scroll from Cave IV which may be older than any other scroll identified thus far. Frank M. Cross of Harvard, who has made a careful study of the script and compared it with the script of other ancient scrolls (this is the science of paleography), is of the opinion that this scroll is to be dated at least two hundred years before the time of

Christ.[3] The technical designation for this scroll is 4QSam[b]. Cross thinks this may have been one of the master scrolls brought to Qumran when the community was first founded. In addition to its antiquity, the scroll is significant because it represents the kind of Hebrew text that was used in the preparation of the earliest Greek translation of the Bible and thus differs from the Masoretic text, which has been mentioned above in the discussion of the Isaiah scrolls from Cave I.

There is one other scroll from Qumran which may be as old as the Samuel scroll. It is a scroll of Exodus (4QEx[f]). Only one column of the original scroll and a few shreds remain. Cross describes the script as "a proto-cursive type less well known than the formal or book hand." [4] He thinks it is possible that this script is even older than that of the Samuel scroll, but the peculiarity of the Exodus script makes it difficult to assign a precise date to it.

It may be well to remind the reader at this point that much older fragments have come from the caves at Wadi Murabbaat. In particular, Murabbaat has produced a papyrus palimpsest (a document reused after the original script has been rubbed out) that is several centuries older than the Samuel fragments from Cave IV of Qumran. Several names and numbers appear on this palimpsest in a script which is probably to be dated in either the seventh or the eighth century B.C. The script which was erased is dim but visible, and Cross thinks that it may belong to approximately the same period.

Have Any Scrolls from Cave XI Been Unrolled?

An Associated Press news release published in the *New York Times* on February 8, 1962, indicated that the Psalms scroll had

[3] Frank M. Cross, Jr., *The Ancient Library of Qumran*, p. 42. This scroll is represented in fragmentary form. The layman should not envision a large, well-preserved scroll but rather some very small pieces which nonetheless indicate the presence of this Samuel scroll at Qumran at a very early date.

[4] *Ibid.*, pp. 42-43.

been unrolled. This same report said that the scroll contains thirty-six psalms plus some additional texts in Hebrew. The exact nature of these additional texts has not been revealed. The news release did state, however, that one of these psalms, number 151, had hitherto been found only in the Greek version of the Bible. If this is true, the Psalms scroll from Cave XI, along with a Samuel scroll from Cave IV (4QSamᵃ) —not to be confused with 4QSamᵇ, mentioned above—would provide additional support for the textual family that is represented in the Septuagint, or Greek version of the Bible.

The *Christian Century* for March 28, 1962, carried additional information about the Psalms scroll from Cave XI. According to this notice released by Frank Brown of Yale University, the tightly rolled scroll had to be subjugated to a "steam-bath temperature" before it could be unrolled, and even then it required six days of careful labor before the task was completed. The announcement added that the present scroll would seem to be the final unit of a two- or three-scroll volume.[5]

What About the Manual of Discipline and the Damascus Document?

The Manual of Discipline (1QS), which might more accurately be called "The Rule (or Order) of the Community," and the Damascus Document (CD) are so important that they will serve as primary sources for our subsequent chapters dealing with the life and the beliefs of the sectarian Jews who produced the Dead Sea Scrolls. Very briefly, we can say here that the Manual of Discipline describes in some detail the procedure to be followed by those who wish to enter into the sectarian way of life. It speaks of examinations, the handling of wealth, seating arrangements when the sectarians were eating, common meals, study, work, and organizational matters. Punishments

[5] P. 406.

for various offenses are listed, and the conflict between the two spirits of truth and error are considered at length.

The Damascus Document has been known since the early part of this century. Widely known among scholars as the Zadokite Fragments, they were found in 1896 in the genizah of a Karaite synagogue in Old Cairo, Egypt. Solomon Schechter published these two incomplete manuscripts in 1910, and the scholarly world became better acquainted with an exclusive group of Jews who considered themselves to be the true remnant of Israel. The Cairo fragments are usually dated between the tenth and the twelfth centuries A.D., but there is now good reason to believe they reflect the very same type of sectarian Judaism that is revealed in the Manual of Discipline.

In fact, the Damascus Document tells about a teacher of righteousness and a select group of people who entered into a new covenant in the land of Damascus. These covenanters, like the Qumran sectarians, were dedicated to the law, and required strict obedience to its demands. Sabbath activities are discussed in detail so that the members knew which things were forbidden. Offerings, dietary rules, procedure for enrolling people in the camps, and the responsibilities of the camp superintendent are all discussed much as these same matters are discussed in the Manual of Discipline. And in both documents we see that the people were looking forward to the imminent coming of God's judgment upon Belial.

Add to these interesting similarities in thought and community organization the fact that fragments of the Damascus Document have been found in Cave IV, and we are led to conclude that the prototype for the Cairo Damascus Document may have come from this very Qumran sect. It is even possible that the "land of Damascus" mentioned in the Damascus Document is really a veiled reference to the wilderness of Judea around Qumran.

We shall return to these two documents when we come to a discussion of the life and beliefs of the people of Qumran.

How Old Are These Scrolls?

William Foxwell Albright, a professor at the Johns Hopkins University, whose ability as an archaeologist and skill as a scholar of Semitics is well known, once remarked that the heated debate over the chronology of the scrolls had actually achieved the proportions of a veritable *guerre des savants*. One scholar in particular, Solomon Zeitlin of Dropsie College in Philadelphia, is willing to assume primary responsibility for this war of the scholars. Zeitlin says, "Indeed, it fell upon me to fire the first shot in this 'war.' " [6]

Zeitlin argues that the scrolls are medieval in origin not ancient as most scholars suppose. Briefly stated, his objections to an early date are as follows: (1) The title "Teacher of Righteousness" was first coined in the middle ages. (2) Commentaries on biblical books were not produced prior to the destruction of the second Temple. (3) The scribe who produced 1QIs* did not know Hebrew very well, and thus committed gross errors in copying his manuscript. Moreover, the very physical appearance of this scroll suggests a relatively late date. (4) Such cardinal ideas of the Essenes and Christians as immortality of the soul, a doctrine of rewards and punishments after death, and the resurrection of the body are not to be found in this medieval literature. (5) The practice of using ellipses to indicate missing words in a text is a late practice, as is the practice of drawing a line through an incorrect word. (6) The addition of certain consonants to assist the reader who is faced with a text having no vowels in it—a practice which we meet in 1QIs*—plus final forms for certain Hebrew letters also indicate that the scrolls could not be as early as is normally claimed.

No one denies the great learning of Zeitlin, especially in the field of Rabbinic studies, but he stands almost alone in this particular dispute. Archaeological evidence that Qumran was de-

---

[6] Solomon Zeitlin, *The Dead Sea Scrolls and Modern Scholarship*, "The Jewish Quarterly Review Monograph Series, No. III" (Philadelphia: Dropsie College, 1956), p. v.

stroyed around A.D. 68, plus the finding in the ruins of Qumran of a jar which is like the scroll jars of Cave I, suggests that the scrolls belonged to people who lived at Qumran until shortly before the destruction of the Temple in A.D. 70.

Paleographical studies are also extremely valuable in dating the scrolls. Now that we have dated documents from the caves at Murabbaat (a number of letters, contracts, deeds, and other documents which can be dated precisely because the date of writing is actually given), it is easy to see that the early second-century script of these Murabbaat documents is considerably later than the script of the Qumran scrolls. Cross states that the science of paleography, as it is now practiced in connection with the Dead Sea Scrolls, is so precise that specialists can date Qumran manuscripts within an interval of one-half century.

With a strong warning that the following dates are not absolutely and infallibly fixed, we list some of the scrolls we have been discussing, along with suggested dates. These are not the dates of composition (unless in the case of some of the commentaries we have a first edition), but rather the dates when our scrolls were copied.

Name of Scroll	Technical Designation	Date
1. St. Mark's Isaiah scroll	1QIs⁴	125-100 B.C.
2. Manual of Discipline	1QS	100-75 B.C.
3. Damascus Document	4QCD (?)	100-63 B.C. (?)
4. Hebrew University Isaiah scroll	1QIs⁵	100-50 B.C.
5. Thanksgiving Psalms	1QH	100-50 B.C.
6. Habakkuk Commentary	1QpHab	25 B.C.-A.D. 25
7. Nahum Commentary	4QpNah	(?)
8. War scroll	1QM	50 B.C.-A.D. 50
9. A Genesis Apocryphon	1QGen Apoc	25 B.C.-A.D. 50

10. Copper scroll   3QInv

                              (?)   A.D. 25-100 (?)

Have We Now Discussed All the Scrolls from Qumran?

By no means! Almost four hundred scrolls are represented at Cave IV alone. About seventy-five different works are known from Cave I. What we have done is to examine a few of the better-known scrolls. Hopefully, those scrolls have been included which have occasioned interest, and perhaps even anxiety, in the minds of lay people. We will now turn our attention to the people of Qumran to consider their way of life and their faith.

V

The Qumran Community

What Was the Origin of the People of Qumran?

BEFORE DISCUSSING THE ORIGIN OF THE PEOPLE OF QUMRAN, IT will be helpful to review briefly the history of the Hebrew people from the time of Moses. It was in the thirteenth century B.C. that Moses led the people of Israel out of Egyptian bondage and brought them together as a covenanted people. In response to the divine initiative which had delivered them from the hands of their oppressors, these Israelites freely chose to enter into a kind of family relationship where God was the awesome senior member and they, by God's election, were to be his responsible children. God's requirement of his children was obedience—obedience to the law which they were privileged to receive through Moses. They must never forsake this law or compromise their faith. They were God's people and they must live accordingly. This responsibility might become burdensome, but this was Israel's mission. She must bear witness to the God who delivered her and made her a nation.

The history of the Hebrew people is actually a story of their struggle to be obedient. It was very tempting to worship the Baals of Canaan when Israel left the wilderness and attempted to make a living from the land. Assyrian gods were very attractive when that great power controlled the Near East. And many a Hebrew was tempted to deny his faith and his God when he saw his Temple in ruins and the Babylonians in charge.

75

Why not accept the gods of the conqueror whose hanging gardens and Ishtar Gate were so impressive? Then came the Persians and the Greeks, each with his culture and way of life, and each time Israel fought anew the battle of faith versus culture. Would she compromise or stand firm in the faith of Moses?

Israel's famous prophets helped the Hebrews see the dangers and the limitations of alien cultures and foreign religions. At their best, they understood that for Israel there could be but one God. Elijah defied both King Ahab and Queen Jezebel as he condemned the prophets of Baal. Hosea remembered the Exodus, the wilderness, Moses and the covenant, and realized that the Israel of the eighth century was a faithless wife who had abandoned her God and compromised her faith. When catastrophe befell the nation and Jerusalem lay in ruins, Ezekiel came forth to warn the Hebrews in Babylonian exile of the dangers of adulterating their faith; and out of the political subjugation a chastened but strong Judaism began to emerge. Ezra re-emphasized the importance of the law for God's people, and once more the integrity of the Hebrew faith seemed to be preserved.

A very severe test, however, lay ahead. Aristotle's pupil, Alexander the Great, was not content with mere political domination. He wanted to spread Greek culture to his conquered lands. After his death part of his empire was subdivided between the Ptolemies in Egypt and the Seleucids who ruled over Mesopotamia and Syria. Both the Ptolemies and the Seleucids were determined to bring Greek culture to Palestine, while many of the loyal and pious Jews of Palestine were just as determined to resist this process of Hellenization, especially if it included a command to worship Zeus and recognize the divinity of the Syrian ruler.

It was during the reign of an ambitious Syrian king, Antiochus IV (175-163 B.C.), who is also called Antiochus Epiphanes because of his claim to be god manifest, that the bitter hostility between the Jews and the Syrians known as the Maccabean Revolt began. Antiochus' taxation was oppressive, but his decision to interfere with the religion of the Jews led directly to bloodshed. Antiochus decreed that the Torah was to be burned wherever it was found. Mothers who had had their children circumcised were put to death along with their children, their families, and those who had actually performed the circumcision. Sabbath observance and the possession of the Torah were regarded as capital offenses, and many Jews died as martyrs rather than eat unclean food. To enforce his program, Antiochus sent his troops to Jerusalem. These troops desecrated the Temple by erecting an altar to Zeus in the Temple court and offering thereon a sacrifice of swine's flesh.

The Maccabean Revolt actually began in the little community of Modein, located a few miles northwest of Jerusalem. A Syrian representative of Antiochus demanded that the Jews pay tribute and offer sacrifice to the pagan deity. When one Jew stepped forth to comply, another infuriated Jew, Mattathias, killed both the compromising Jew and the Syrian officer.

It was at this juncture in Jewish history that a group of loyal and pious Jews known as Hasidim arose. These men were like Elijah, for they would rather die than forsake their Mosaic heritage and their Torah. They would not accept Antiochus' program of Hellenization. They would not forget their law. It was probably one of these Hasidim who wrote the book of Daniel and encouraged his compatriots to show both courage and faith in the face of the suffering and persecution symbolized by a fiery furnace and a lion's den. It was this same Hasidic author who had his heroes, Shadrach, Meshach, and Abednego, tell Nebuchadnezzar that the Hebrew God would protect them, "But if not, be it known to you, O king, that we will not serve your gods or worship the golden image which you have set up" (Dan. 3:18).

It was probably these very Hasidim who became the spiritual

ancestors of the Qumran sectarians. The precise relationship is not yet clear, but it seems safe to say that the sectarians were either an element within the Hasidic movement or descendants of it.

When Did These Sectarians Move to Qumran?

Unfortunately, an easy answer to this question is not possible. If the figures mentioned in the Dead Sea Scrolls could be identified with historic personages whose places in history are well known, the task would be simplified. As yet, however, the available evidence is susceptible to divergent interpretations by the scholars. Even the word "descendants," which has been used above to describe the relationship between the Hasidim and the sectarians, may be misleading. It is possible that the sect represented a wing of the general Hasidic movement and that its inception must be traced back to the very beginning of the second century B.C., but again this does not tell us when the sectarians moved to Qumran.

Five archaeological expeditions to excavate Khirbet Qumran have produced evidence which helps fix the period when the buildings at Qumran were first constructed and inhabited. We know, for instance, that Qumran was built on the ruined foundations of a sixth-century Israelite fortress. It is difficult to date the preliminary installations with precision, but an abundance of coins does enable us to make educated guesses about the construction dates for the major building program at Qumran.

There are, for instance, fifteen copper coins from the reign of John Hyrcanus (134-104 B.C.) ; eighty-six from the reign of Alexander Janneus (103-76 B.C.) ; only five from the days of Herod the Great (37-4 B.C.) ; and then, ascending in number, sixty from the period of Agrippa I (A.D. 37-44) ; and seventy-eight from the period of the first Jewish revolt. After this period, there is such a marked decrease in the number of coins found that the archaeologists cite this fact as evidence that Qumran was probably destroyed in A.D. 68 by the soldiers of Vespasian.[1]

While A.D. 68 may be accepted as the date for the destruction of Qumran, our original question has not yet been answered. When did these sectarians move to Qumran? The wealth of coins from the reign of Janneus suggests an occupation of this site during his reign. Allegro is convinced that Janneus is the Wicked Priest mentioned in the Habakkuk Commentary and again in the Nahum Commentary as the Lion of Wrath. If Allegro's evidence were compelling, it could be argued that the Teacher of Righteousness, who was a contemporary of the Wicked Priest, must have been at Qumran during the reign of Janneus. But, as we have already learned from the earlier discussion of these two commentaries, there is no textual proof that Allegro is correct in his interpretation.

If Simon (143-134 B.C.) were the Wicked Priest, as Cross believes, the date for the Teacher of Righteousness could be moved back half a century and still not be in conflict with the archaeological evidence provided by the coins. It is certainly possible that the Teacher of Righteousness was so disturbed by the priestly pretensions of Jonathan (160-143 B.C.) and Simon that he took his little band of followers and fled to the wilderness in the hope that he, like Moses, might be instrumental in maintaining the true Israel ruled by an undefiled Zadokite priesthood. If Jonathan and Simon both wanted to be high priests, there was nothing else for the dissenting Teacher of Righteousness to do but establish a rival community and priesthood at Qumran.

The fact is that we cannot answer our question with either

---

[1] The sparsity of coins during the reign of Herod the Great plus the evidence of damage caused by an earthquake which secular sources date in 31 B.C. lead scholars to believe that Qumran was uninhabited for slightly more than a quarter of a century during the latter part of Herod's reign (37-4 B.C.). Cross says that the fundamental plan of the site was not changed when it was rebuilt and that there is no doubt that the people who resettled Qumran were the same as those who lived there prior to the earthquake.

precision or certainty. Even if the date of the Teacher of Righteousness could be established, we would not be sure that he
was the original leader and founder of the Qumran sect. About
all that can be said is that by the end of the second century B.C.
a priestly community had been established at Qumran and its
inhabitants were busy copying scriptures. Both the coins and
the script of the St. Mark's Isaiah scroll (1QIsᵃ) serve as evidence for such a conclusion.

Were the People of Qumran Celibates?

There is considerable evidence that a vast majority of the
men living at Qumran were unmarried. First, the fact that there
is no explicit reference to either women or children in the
Manual of Discipline can be cited. (There is a reference to
"bearing seed," but the meaning of this phrase is unclear.) In
a manual that gives as many detailed prescriptions for the order-
ing of community life as are found in the Manual of Discipline,
it would be a little surprising to have no references to women
and children if, as a matter of fact, they were present in the
community.

Excavations of the graves in the three cemeteries (one large
and two small ones) at Qumran have turned up female skeletons, but only one of these female skeletons came from the
main cemetery which contained about one thousand bodies.
The other female skeletons, along with the skeletons of children, came from the two smaller cemeteries.

There are several ways to account for the presence of these
female skeletons. It may be that they represent the women
who came to Qumran as the wives of the original members of
the sect. Future members may have remained celibate. Or, it is
possible that the attitude of the sect changed and that, in the
latter period of the sect's stay at Qumran, marriage was permitted. One hypothesis which accounts for these burials is that
a few saintly women may have come to Qumran and asked for

the privilege of being buried in this area hallowed by the dedication of the sectarians to the law.

Whereas celibacy seems to have been the rule among the Qumran sectarians, it is likely that some of the sectarians did marry. We must not confuse the few hundred people who lived at Qumran with the larger membership outside Qumran. Estimates of the number of people who lived at Qumran vary, but 500 people for any given period would have been a maximum number, and it may be that 150 to 200 would be a more realistic estimate. The larger group outside Qumran may have numbered in the thousands. Assuming that the sectarians were either Essenes (to be explained below) or related to the Essenes, the total membership might be four thousand or more.

Both the Damascus Document and the Rule of the Congregation mention women and children. The Rule of the Congregation consists of two columns of material found in Cave I at Qumran. While it appears that these two columns belong to the roll known as the Manual of Discipline, it is also clear that the Rule of the Congregation represents an independent composition. It is not known whether the Rule describes another stage in the sect's history or whether it envisions life as it will be in the future, but when all the evidence is considered, there seems little doubt that there was a marrying group of sectarians. If some of the married members lived close to Qumran, this might account for the female skeletons in the cemeteries. Our original answer, however, still stands. A majority of the sectarians living at Qumran were celibate.

What Were the Entrance Requirements for Admission into the Qumran Community?

There was a very definite procedure to be followed by those who wished to gain admission to the community at Qumran. First, there had to be a desire to obey the law of Moses as it was interpreted by the sect. This presupposed that the candidate was unhappy with the form and practice of religion which existed in Palestine apart from the Jews represented by the Qumran sect. The candidate had probably already heard rumors about the rigor and discipline which prevailed among the Qumran sectarians, and was convinced that this strict adherence to the law was essential if the Mosaic heritage was to be maintained in its integrity. He may well have been prepared to believe that the Qumran community represented the elect of God and the true Israel. Dissatisfied with the popular forms of religion, the candidate was willing to take his property and move to the wilderness.

Due to the fact that the Manual of Discipline appears to be a composite of material, it is not easy to state the exact order of events in the long probation program which preceded full admission into the sect. According to Burrows, the candidate first took a strict oath of allegiance to the law of Moses. Obedience to this law was the heart of the Qumran movement, so it may well be that the first step for the prospective member was to swear his loyalty to the law as it was interpreted and understood at Qumran.

After taking his oath, the candidate underwent an examination conducted by the inspector or examiner. If the candidate appeared to have sufficient wisdom and understanding to comprehend instruction and succeed as a member of the community, he was accepted as a postulant and given preliminary information about the goals, practices, and doctrines of the sect. The Manual of Discipline does not state the exact length of this period of postulancy, but it may have continued for as long as a year.

We do know that at the end of this period of postulancy the candidate appeared before the full-fledged members of the community for examination. If they were satisfied with his conduct and progress, they admitted him to the next stage of probation; conversely, if they were not satisfied, the candidate was rejected.

If the vote was favorable, the candidate moved into what we

may call a novicehood or novitiate. At this point he could become a member of the council of the community and move one step closer to full membership. This entailed a one-year period of probation, during which the candidate neither shared the purity (perhaps a reference to participation in the sacred rites and meals) nor the wealth of the full-fledged members. His association with the members was undoubtedly more intimate during this period than it was while he was still a postulant, but there were still more requirements to be met. There was another examination at the end of his first year as a novice, and if the candidate was once more successful he entered into the third and final stage of his probation.

This last stage consisted of an additional year as a novice. As he entered upon the second year of his novitiate, he turned over his wealth to the overseer of the sect. This property was not yet to be used by the membership as a whole. (We can conjecture that the wealth was held in the candidate's name until it was finally decided whether he was eligible for full membership within the sect.) During the last stage, the candidate had to be willing to donate his services to the community, but he was still not permitted to participate in the sacred drink or common meal of these new covenanters.

It was only after a successful postulancy and novitiate that the candidate was ready for his final initiation into the community. The exact nature of the final rite of initiation is not clear, but it may be at this time that the candidate declared his hatred for all those of stubborn heart who refused to join the community of God's elect at Qumran. He may have dedicated himself to a life of righteousness and justice and indicated his desire to bring like-minded men into this new covenant of steadfast love. He may have been required to promise that he would observe the festivals according to the times established by the special solar calendar in use at Qumran, and remain true to his vows even though he was faced by dread and terror.

Having thus committed himself to the ways of the sect, the

83

candidate entered the water to be ceremonially cleansed in preparation for his participation in the purity of the full-fledged members. He was warned that mere washing was of no value unless it was accompanied by true repentance. If he repented, obeyed God's word, and separated himself from the wicked who had forsaken the law, he was worthy to be a member of the community.

What Was the Nature of Life Within the Community?

The Qumran community was organized according to a hierarchical system, each man ranked according to his knowledge and performance of the law. At the annual review a man's status and rank might change, but once the rank and order was established it had to be observed. The priestly sons of Zadok were the leaders of this community. These priests offered the blessings when new men were entering the covenant. The priests blessed the bread and wine before the members ate, and whenever ten men of the council of the community were present there had to be a priest among them. When the members came together for a meeting, the priests were to be seated first, followed by the elders, and finally by the rest of the men seated in strict accordance to their rank.

Democracy prevailed in this order. Any man could speak his opinion as long as he observed rank. He could not speak out of turn and he could not interrupt the speaker, but in his proper time he would be heard. Even the priests were not exempt from examination in the annual review. When problems arose within the community, they had to be brought before the entire membership and voted on. If two of the members had a difference of opinion, they were to settle it peacefully and privately if at all possible. If it became necessary to call the matter to the attention of the community as a whole, the evidence had to be produced in proper order and there had to be witnesses that the two men had tried to settle their quarrel privately.

The word "community" has been chosen purposely in this

chapter because it appears frequently in the Manual of Discipline and suggests a tightly knit group of men dedicated to the same goals, practicing the same faith, and embracing a common hope. These were men who ate together, worshiped together, and took counsel together. They were united by their common dislike for the Jerusalem priesthood and by their conviction that they were the remnant who would preserve the faith and be the heart of the new covenant. Here in the wilderness the true Israel, which had its beginning with Moses in another wilderness, would be maintained.

Much time was devoted to studying the law, a fact which is obvious because of the multitude of Torah fragments which have come from Cave IV. These sectarians were so committed to the law that at least one man was busy studying it day and night. Wherever there were ten men, they were to take turns studying the law so that there would never be a moment during the day or the night when the law was not being considered.

As a result of archaeological work, something is known about the very room where the sectarians busied themselves copying the laws and other writings that seemed important to them. This scriptorium was about forty-three feet long and thirteen feet wide. Fastened to its floor was a long, narrow table measuring about sixteen feet in length and eighteen to twenty inches in height. Near this table were low benches attached to the wall. Even the inkwells of the scribes were not completely destroyed. Some were made of terra-cotta and others of bronze. The dried ink found in these inkwells has been analyzed and found to be of carbon composition, a composition similar to that of the ink used in the making of the scrolls. A desk top that has been reconstructed has two small, shallow, bowl-shaped depressions at the top, suggesting to some scholars that the scribes were equipped with finger bowls for cleansing their hands prior to copying their scriptures, or perhaps just prior to writing the divine name.

Additional information about the daily life in Qumran is

forthcoming from the ruins. The past comes alive as basalt mills, storage silos for grain, elaborate water supply systems with conduits, cisterns, and pools, and the remains of pottery are found. More than a thousand pieces of neatly stacked dinnerware have been uncovered in what must have been the pantry at Qumran. Cups and bowls, plates and pitchers, wine flasks, and serving dishes have now come to light, along with the kitchen and the ovens. Even the toilet facilities of Qumran have not escaped the attention of the excavators.

One of the most curious discoveries of the archaeologists is the carefully buried bones of many animals. The bones of cattle, sheep, and goats were packed neatly in jars or between large pieces of jars, thereby suggesting that special significance was attached to these burials. Some scholars think these are the bones from the meat eaten at the regular sacred meals of the sect, but the number of burials is scarcely sufficient to make this hypothesis plausible. More likely is Milik's suggestion—that these are bones from meat eaten on the occasion of the annual review, which may have come at the same time of year as the Jewish Festival of Weeks (Christian Pentecost). Regardless of which hypothesis we accept, one thing is clear: The sectarians were not vegetarians.

Were the Sectarians Punished for Infractions of the Rules?

In columns six and seven of the Manual of Discipline are listed a number of punishments for those who failed to abide by the rules of the community. If a man consciously lied about his wealth, he was excluded from the purity of the many (again we take this phrase to mean exclusion from the most intimate association of the full-fledged members and their sacred meals) for a period of one year, and he was deprived of one fourth of his food ration. This enforced fasting would certainly have been severe if the bones mentioned above represent the remains of the meat eaten by the sectarians at their regular meals over a period of a century or even a half century.

If a member failed to keep the law recorded in Deuteronomy, which commanded the faithful man to fear the glorious and awful name of the Lord, he was to be punished for an unspecified length of time. (It would be well to remember at this point that there are still Jewish people who think it improper to speak the actual name of God, and circumvent it by such a phrase as "the Name.") [2]

Other offenses included an argumentative spirit which caused a breakdown of the fellowship between a man and his neighbor. Or again, the dignity of the priest in the community is indicated by the fact that a member who intentionally cursed a priest was to be punished for a period of one year and excluded from the inner circle of the membership.

Lying, bearing false witness against a neighbor, fraud, vindictiveness, vulgar speech, the interruption of a member while he was speaking, and sleeping at public meetings (an official session of the full-fledged members) were all punishable offenses. And apparently the heat of the wilderness tempted some of the sectarians to disrobe, because one listed punishment for six months' duration was reserved for the man who walked naked in the presence of a neighbor. Spitting, indecent exposure, and foolish laughter were strictly forbidden. Complaints against the community were far more serious than complaints against individual members, but both offenses could bring exclusion on either a temporary or a permanent basis.[3]

Did the Sectarians Own Private Property?

The evidence is ambiguous on this point. There are statements in the Manual of Discipline which would lead one to

[2] T. H. Gaster's translation of this same passage indicates that the punishment is permanent exclusion from the sect. Cf. *The Dead Sea Scriptures in English Translation* (Garden City, N. Y.: Doubleday & Co., Inc., 1956), p. 52.

[3] Cf. Josephus, *Wars of the Jews*, II, viii, 9, for somewhat similar regulations and rules for the Essenes. Josephus says that the Essenes avoided spitting in a public meeting, and were careful not to expose their bodies, even during easement, lest they "afront the divine rays of light." Also see Exod. 20:26.

believe that the candidate for membership had to turn over all his property before he could be fully admitted into membership. We have even seen that it was a serious offense if a man lied about his wealth. On the other hand, it was equally clear in the Damascus Document that a member was not required to turn over all his wealth, but was enjoined to contribute two days' wages per month to support the work of the community.

Nor is the ambiguity simply between the Manual of Discipline and the Damascus Document. The internal witness of the Manual is not quite clear. We are told, for instance, that the candidate for membership had to bring his knowledge, his strength, and his wealth into the community; and when he entered upon the last stage of his probation, we are again told that he had to relinquish his wealth to the overseer. The difficulty comes in the list of punishments where we read that a member who has defrauded the community must repay in full. If he is unable to make restitution, he is to be separated from the purity of the many for a period of sixty days. Father Sutcliffe, who is professor of Hebrew and Old Testament at Heythrop College in Great Britain, would resolve this problem by saying that the Hebrew word describing the restitution does not necessarily mean the payment of a monetary fine, but merely suggests that an appropriate nonmonetary compensation was required. But, as Chaim Rabin of the Hebrew University in Jerusalem notes, any kind of restitution or payment would seem to presuppose private ownership.

The absence of coins in the caves at Qumran must also be remembered. More than 750 coins have been found at Khirbet Qumran, but thus far not one of these has come from the caves where some of the sectarians may have lived. It may be, of course, that it is simply a coincidence that coins have not yet been found in the area where the people actually lived, but the available evidence suggests that all money was kept within the confines of the community center. This evidence is often cited by those who are convinced that private property was not permitted at Qumran.

The curious discovery of 558 coins, which had been hidden away in three jars, still puzzles the experts. Most, if not all these silver coins, come from the first century B.C. and may have been hidden in the ruins of Qumran just prior to its rebuilding for the last time. Perhaps a prospective member decided to conceal a portion of his wealth, or perhaps—and this would seem somewhat more likely—a superintendent hid the money for safekeeping either for himself (!) or for the community. The case of the silver coins is simply another mystery which has not yet been solved.

Did the Sectarians Have a Special Calendar?

S. Talmon of the Hebrew University in Jerusalem believes that the calendar controversy between the Qumran sectarians and the Jerusalem priesthood was a decisive factor in the formation of the Qumran community. Devout Jews had resented the attempts of Antiochus Epiphanes to "change the times and the law" (Dan. 7:25), and it may well be that Judaism itself became divided on this issue. In fact, T. H. Gaster of Columbia University and Dropsie College describes the calendar controversy as a "regular bone of contention" among the Jews. It can also be noted in this connection that anyone wishing to enter the Qumran community was required to promise he would neither advance nor postpone the times of the festivals and seasons as established by the community.

While we cannot be certain about the exact time of origin for the calendar used at Qumran, it is fairly certain that the Qumran calendar was a solar calendar of 364 days. Dates for festivals and seasons calculated on the basis of this solar calendar would definitely differ from those set forth by the Jerusalem priesthood on the basis of a lunar calendar. This fact may explain why the Habakkuk Commentary refers to the Wicked Priest as coming to Qumran to enter into controversy with them on *their* sabbath rest. What we would have, then, would be two rival priesthoods following different calendrical systems and celebrating a given festival at different times of the year.

Christians are interested in the matter of the Qumran calendar because they wonder if it might shed light on the date of the Last Supper. The Synoptic Gospels (Matthew, Mark, and Luke) seem to indicate that the Last Supper was a Passover meal, but the Fourth Gospel says that the Last Supper took place before the Passover. The suggestion has now been made that Jesus and his disciples followed the Qumran calendar and celebrated the Passover on Tuesday evening rather than on Thursday evening, as is commonly supposed. If this hypothesis is correct, an apparent inconsistency among the Gospels would be resolved. Milik, however, warns against a too hasty acceptance of this solution by reminding us that only once in every thirty years would the Qumran Passover have fallen in the same week as the official Passover.

Were the Qumran Sectarians Essenes?

In the earlier days of scrolls research, there was considerable hesitancy to answer an unqualified "yes" to this question. Careful scholars pointed out that the accounts of the Essenes given by Flavius Josephus, Pliny the Elder, and Philo Judaeus could not be made to agree exactly with the description of the sectarians which is found in the Manual of the Discipline and the Damascus Document. Many of these same scholars were willing to admit that the sectarians resembled the Essenes, but they were not willing to equate the two groups.

Today the pendulum is swinging slowly toward an Essene identification of the Qumran sect. Kurt Schubert, professor of Jewish religion and culture at the University of Vienna, probably represents the majority opinion when he concludes that the sectarians must be included in the broad complex of Essene groups. In this conclusion, Schubert seems to recognize that there may have been more Essenes than those described by such early writers as Josephus, Pliny, and Philo. In other words, it is not essential that the sectarians fit exactly the descriptions of the Essenes given by these authorities because each of them may simply have been describing that form of the Essene movement which he happened to know. It may well be that the Dead Sea Scrolls provide as valuable a description of the Essenes as can be found in any of these other sources. This is the reason I have chosen in this chapter to first discuss life at Qumran and then turn to the question of the Essenes at the end of the chapter.

It is the Jewish historian Josephus (A.D. 37-?100) who gives us the most detailed account of the Essenes. In his autobiography, Josephus tells us that he came from "not an ignoble" family and that he was so famous for his memory and understanding that at the age of fourteen the high priests and principle men of Jerusalem sought him out in order to get his accurate interpretation of the law. Such modesty, along with the fact that Josephus switched from a position of leadership of Jewish forces to a position of close friendship with the Roman emperor Vespasian, suggests that his account of history should be read with caution; nevertheless, his account of the Essenes may be fairly accurate because he claims to have been a member of this sect for a time.

According to Josephus, there were three groups of Jews: Sadducees, Pharisees, and Essenes. The Essenes, about four thousand in number, are described by Josephus as a very righteous and virtuous group of Jews who had all things in common. No member of the sect had more than another member. The rich man and the poor man shared equally in the common property of the group. Servants were not kept, but each member was deeply concerned for the well-being of his neighbor. Some Essenes did not marry. This was not because they regarded sexual relationships as evil in themselves, but because they were convinced that women were unfaithful! There were other Essenes who did marry.

Josephus says that some of the Essenes considered oil to be a defilement of the skin, whereas perspiration was a good thing. Continence and restraint of passion were admirable qualities, as were love of truth and dedication to the law. These Essenes prayed regularly, worked diligently, and sometimes lived to be a hundred years of age because of their simple diet and their regular schedule. When an Essene left one community to travel to another, he did not need to take anything along other than a weapon to protect himself from robbers and thieves. It was the responsibility of the group he was visiting to provide whatever clothes and food he might need.

As far as beliefs were concerned, these Essenes tended to ascribe all things to God and die without fear because they believed in the immortality of the soul. They gave up their souls willingly, as though they expected to receive them again. They believed in assisting the righteous and hating the wicked. Not even torture was an excuse for revealing the secret truths of the sect to outsiders.

After morning work, the members came in from their tasks (each man did that type of work in which he had some skill), clothed themselves in white, bathed in cold water, sat down to a common meal presided over by priests who said grace both before and after the meal, ate their bread and the one other kind of food which they had, and prepared to return to their work. Supper was a repetition of the same procedure. As with the Qumran sectarians, the Essenes spoke quietly and in turn.

Pliny (A.D. 23-79), a Roman naturalist and author, adds the very interesting observation that a group of Essenes lived apart from the world on the west side of the Dead Sea just far enough removed from that body of water to escape its noxious odors.[4]

---

[4] The exact meaning of Pliny's "noxious exhalations" is uncertain. It is possible that he is here describing the Essene eagerness to separate themselves from the harmful things of the world, but the context seems to favor some such interpretation as that given above.

He adds the further geographical note that the town of Engedi was formerly located below (the precise meaning of the original text is not clear at this point) this people. Pliny goes on to say that these Essenes had neither women nor money. They were strangers to sexual desire. The palm trees were their only companions. There were no births among them, but their sect continued to increase in membership because of the considerable number of converts who came to them to escape the "weariness" of life which they experienced outside the sect.

Philo, an Alexandrian Jew who lived and wrote at about the same time as Jesus of Nazareth, praises the moral excellence of the Essenes. Philo says that they lived in villages rather than in cities to avoid the iniquities of the city dwellers. Some of them were farmers; others were craftsmen. They did not hoard gold and silver and they did not strive to own large tracts of land. They were pacifists who were content and happy in their way of life. Much of their time, especially on the sabbaths, was spent in the study of ethics and the law. They abstained from oaths and shared their goods, though Philo does make it clear that they may have kept some of their wages.

As we consider these classical descriptions of the Essenes and compare them with what we know about the Qumran sectarians, we notice both similiarities and differences. One major difference is the stress placed upon the new covenant by the sectarians. This note is lacking in both Philo and Josephus. Moreover, the sectarians were obviously looking forward to the coming of two Messiahs, but we fail to find this same emphasis among the Essenes as they are described by the classical writers. Nor do these writers stress the Teacher of Righteousness, as did the author of the Habakkuk Commentary. It may also be that Philo's Essenes were more pacifistic than the sectarians who produced the War scroll, but here we must be prepared to admit that the sectarian attitude may have changed across the years. Perhaps pacifists in the present age can be prepared to fight at the end, when they think God's judgment is being visited upon the wicked sons of darkness.

The similarities between the Essenes and the sectarians are obvious and striking. Pliny's mention of Essenes living on the west side of the Dead Sea speaks strongly for an identification of the two groups. It does not seem likely that two important and distinct groups would live so close together in the Qumran area. Both the Essenes and the sectarians shared common property, ate common meals, observed rank and order, stressed the study of the law, and strove for moral and ritual purity. In both organizations the priests played the most important roles, saying the graces, blessing the food, and acting as leaders. There is even a marked similarity between the superintendent of the sectarian organization and the steward of the Essenes, each being responsible for the income and property which was left in his trust. Add to these similarities the possibility that many Essenes were celibate, as were the men of the Qumran community, and the further possibility that the probationary periods for entrance into both communities were similar in nature if not in length, and we can see that there certainly are some reasons for relating the Qumran sectarians to the Essenes of Josephus, Pliny, and Philo.[5]

[5] The lay reader should be warned that the above discussion of the Essenes and their relationship to the sectarians is so compressed and condensed as to make a difficult problem seem unduly simple. It is impossible, for instance, to deal with the theory that there never were any Essenes. Nor can there be any discussion of the views of those scholars who would identify the sectarians with the Pharisees (I see a connection here), or the Zealots, or the Christians. It is recommended that the reader who wishes to pursue this study further consult the excellent and balanced treatments of this subject by Millar Burrows in his two books *The Dead Sea Scrolls*, pp. 273-98, and *More Light on the Dead Sea Scrolls*, pp. 228-74.

VI

The Faith at Qumran

What Were the Basic Beliefs of the Qumran Jews?

THE JEWS AT QUMRAN BELIEVED THEY WERE THE ELECT OF God called out to be the members of the new covenant and true Israel. They were the remnant in the wilderness preparing the way of the Lord. The old age was coming to an end. The end of days and a new age were at hand. God and his angels were entering into the final conflict against the forces of Belial and the sons of darkness. Though they were sinners unworthy of the honor, the sectarians believed that God had called them to be the children of light. It would be their privilege to fight for justice, for truth, and for the ultimate defeat of the forces of darkness. It was their privilege to be obedient to the law of Moses and thereby preserve all that was precious and best in Israel's glorious heritage. Not all Jews would participate in God's victory over Belial, but those who left the world and committed themselves to the rigorous discipline and devotion of sectarian life were already sharing in the salvation being procured for them by their God. Life at Qumran was the best possible preparation for life in the new age.

Did the Sectarians Stress God's Sovereignty?

There can be no doubt that the sectarians emphasized the sovereignty of God. He was either directly or indirectly responsible for everything that happened. It was he who had created the spirits of light and darkness and determined the role they would play in the present age. If a man walked in righteousness it was because he was under the dominion of the Prince of Lights. If, on the other hand, a man failed to recognize the demands of the law as these were interpreted by the sectarians, it was obvious that he was under the dominion of the Angel of Darkness. In his unfathomable wisdom God had established a plan for his creation, a plan which was unfolding and moving toward an inevitable conclusion of God's own choosing. Good men should never despair if the judgment seemed to be delayed. The appointed times of God were sure to come.

If such a thoroughgoing emphasis on God's sovereignty seems harsh to us, we should remember its virtues as seen by the eye of faith. First, these sectarians were affirming that the God of Israel was worthy of their complete trust and confidence. In their own way they were singing, "A Mighty Fortress Is Our God." Men would forsake the covenant and fail to be obedient to the laws of God given to Israel through Moses; men would sin and die, but God would endure forever and his purposes would be established.

Secondly, the sectarians were saying something about the nature of history. Men's ideas and actions did not determine what the future would be. Rather, history's meaning was to be discerned in the actions of a righteous and holy God. The God who had acted once in history to deliver their ancestors from oppression in the land of Egypt was once more acting in history to save his people. His covenant of old was being re-established in the lives of the individuals who chose to become members of the sectarian movement. Through this covenanted community, God would act to bring an end to all those who opposed his will, and through this community God was preparing men for the advent of the messianic age.

Were the Sectarians Dualistic?

The sectarians were obviously dualists. The real problem here is to define the precise nature of this dualism. Did the sectarians believe there were two eternal and opposed powers in constant struggle with each other? Was there a realm of darkness which was eternally at odds with another realm of light? If so, could it be said that the Persian religion, with its god of darkness, had exerted influence upon the authors of the Qumran literature?

The Manual of Discipline does contain specific references to two spirits, but it is clear that the sectarian authors thought of God as being the creator of both spirits. The sectarians did not regard these two spirits as eternal and uncreated. Rather, the spirits were always subject to God's control. Only God was sovereign.

The real conflict, as seen in the Manual of Discipline, is between those who want to be obedient to God's will (as set forth in the law and interpreted by the sectarians) and those who reject the sectarian interpretation of God's will. The sectarians may have regarded the priestly pretensions of Alexander Janneus as the actions of an arrogant and wicked man who was dominated by the Angel of Darkness, and therefore considered it their responsibility to oppose him and his way of life with all their strength and determination. They may have felt the same way about the Jerusalem priesthood and all others who refused to join their covenanted group in the wilderness. This dualism separated Jews not only from Syrians and Romans but also from other Jews who did not practice ritual and moral purity in accordance with the sectarian rules.

The source of this conflict is not simply psychological in nature. The Angel of Darkness and the Angel of Light do not represent two psychological temperaments or dispositions. The conflict and dualism do not arise merely from a good inclination and a bad inclination in the hearts of men. This dualism has cosmic dimensions. God's forces in both heaven and earth must fight against the sons of darkness. Both men and angels must participate in the battles which will come at the end of the age. Good men and good angels must fight against bad men and bad angels until God gives the final victory.

What we do not find in the Qumran literature is the Gnostic note that flesh and the material world are evil. These sectarians did not go to Qumran to discipline a body which was essentially evil. They certainly did not regard the Creator God as an evil demiurge who had soiled his hands with the formation of the material world. The sectarians did not distinguish between a spiritual soul which was good and a material body which was evil. There is no evidence that they regarded the soul as a divine spark which was temporarily imprisoned in a body. The sectarians were convinced that they could do the will of God in their own age. Hostile angelic powers might hinder them in their attempts to be obedient to God's will, but there is no evidence that the sectarians wanted to free a spiritual soul from an evil body so that the disembodied soul could worship God more perfectly.

This leaves the question of the Persian religion and the possible influence it may have exerted on the faith of the sectarians. Did the sectarians borrow their terminology from an Iranian background? Zoroastrianism had a god of light (Ahura Mazda) and a god of darkness (Angra Mainyu, or Ahriman), and there was a definite conflict between these two opposing forces. Perhaps this is where the Qumran authors got their ideas about angels of light and darkness.

My immediate reaction to such suggestions is to urge caution in the making of easy comparisons. It may well be that the phrases "Angel of Light," and "Angel of Darkness" came from the Iranian religion and that the light-darkness motif was borrowed from this same religion, but it is certainly not essential to turn to Zoroastrianism to find the source of a dualistic tendency. There is the story of the ninth-century B.C. prophet Micaiah ben Imlah, who opposed the popular prophets who were predicting victory for King Ahab of Israel and King Jehoshaphat of Judah. Micaiah came before the kings and told them they would be defeated if they went up against Ramoth-Gilead. When asked why his prophecy differed from that of the popular prophets, Micaiah explained that it was the Lord's intention to send a lying spirit to act through Zedekiah and entice Ahab to his death on the battlefield. Thus, sectarian theology and thought may have owed much to this Jewish background.

I might also point out that a student of world religions such as John Noss of Franklin and Marshall College admits that the ancient Persian scriptures are something less than clear when they discuss the origin of the evil spirit, Angra Mainyu. Is he the creation of Ahura Mazda or does Ahura Mazda simply discover that where there is good action it is natural to find its opposite? Noss thinks it is the latter view which prevails in the Gathas (Hymns of Zoroaster).[1] Until the exact relationship of Angra Mainyu to Ahura Mazda can be determined, it may be premature to argue that sectarian thought about God's relationship to Belial reflects an Iranian background.

Did the Sectarians Expect a Messiah to Come?

If the Manual of Discipline is used as the source, it seems clear that the sectarians expected two messiahs, one from Aaron and another from Israel. In the ninth column of this scroll are regulations governing the wealth of the holy men. We are told that the wealth of these men was not to be shared or mixed with that wealth belonging to men of deceit. The holy men of the community were obligated to abide strictly by the law and make their judgments in strict conformity with the original rules of the community "until the coming of a prophet and the messiahs of Aaron and Israel."

In analyzing this passage from the scroll, it can be seen that the sectarians expected a prophet and two messiahs to come in the future. The precedent for such a hope can be found in the

[1] John B. Noss, *Man's Religions* (rev. ed.; New York: The Macmillan Company, 1956), pp. 442 ff.

Old Testament. In Deut. 18:18, the Lord promises Moses that a prophet like him will be raised up from among the brethren of the Hebrew people. It seems obvious that the sectarians were still looking forward to the advent of this prophet, and they were convinced that when he came he would be accompanied by a duly anointed high priest and a duly anointed king.

The precedent for two messiahs, one lay and one priestly, can also be found in the Old Testament. In the book of Ezra (see also Zech. 4:14) we read that the priest, Joshua, co-operated with the prince, Zerubbabel, to build the altar of God so that the Jews who were returning to Jerusalem from their exile in Babylon could offer sacrifices to God. These two leaders continued their co-operation in the rebuilding of the Temple, which had been destroyed by the Babylonians in 587 B.C. For reasons unknown, Zerubbabel disappeared suddenly (perhaps the Persian overlords sensed the incipient longing for political independence and decided to eliminate the focal point of such an aspiration), but there can be no doubt that for a time the priest and the prince worked together as joint leaders of the returning Jews. It is also clear that the prophets Haggai and Zechariah thought of Joshua and Zerubbabel as high priest and Davidic prince respectively.

It is when attention is shifted from the Manual of Discipline to the Damascus Document that difficulty in understanding the messianic expectations of the sectarians begins. In three instances the references in the Damascus Document are to a messiah of Aaron and Israel rather than to two messiahs. Scholars have considered emending the text by adding one small letter so that the Damascus Document would also read messiahs, but the finding of another fragment of the Damascus Document in Cave IV, a fragment which gives the singular reading, raises serious question whether or not such an emendation ought to be made. Biblical specialists have suggested a number of ways to solve this particular problem, but the intricacies of these solutions have no place in our present study.

We do know that there were both priests and laymen living at Qumran. It is also clear that the Manual of Discipline does contain references to two messiahs. The determination of the sectarians to keep separate the role of the king and the priest may have prompted them to leave Jerusalem when the sons of Mattathias attempted to combine the two functions.

In the Rule of the Congregation, another aspect of the messianic expectations of the sectarians is discovered. Even though the text of the Rule is incomplete, it is clear that the reference here is to two messiahs rather than to one. These two messiahs were expected to be present at the table of communion at the end of days. On this occasion, the priestly messiah would lead the way into the meeting of the council of the community. He would be followed by all the other priestly descendants of Aaron, who would take their seats before him, each according to his rank. Next, the messiah of Israel would enter, followed by the lay leaders in their respective order and rank. When all had come to the table, the priestly messiah would bless the bread or the wine and then the messiah of Israel would add his blessing. Finally, the entire congregation of the community, each person according to his rank, would offer thanks and then eat.

Scholars are not agreed whether this meal described in the Rule of the Congregation is the actual meal of the sectarians viewed as a liturgical anticipation of the messianic banquet or whether it is a description of the future banquet when the messiah of Israel will be present with the elect. This much, however, is clear: The Rule of the Congregation and the Manual of Discipline both contain references to a priest and a lay messiah who will share the leadership over God's elect in the new age.

What Was the Sectarian Interpretation of the Covenant?

The sectarians believed that the God of Abraham, Isaac, and Jacob was determined to preserve his covenant forever with a remnant of people who would be obedient to his law. Unlike their forefathers, who came out of Egypt into a wilderness where they waited for both the law and the making of the covenant, the sectarians believed that they already had the law and the covenant. They were the true remnant of Israel elected by God's will to become an eternal planting, a community of the faithful through whom God's truth and righteous activity could be made known to the world.

Their covenant was exclusive. Just as the prophet Isaiah's remnant did not include all Israel, so the sectarian concept of the remnant excluded many Jews. Only those Jews who were willing to separate themselves from the nonsectarian world and to be bound by the strict discipline of the community could be members of the covenant. There was no place in this covenant for the rebellious angels and the sons born to them by the daughters of men. The sons of Noah and the descendants of Jacob might also be excluded from membership in the covenanted community. The sectarians blamed the faithlessness of their Jewish brethren as being the cause of the Egyptian bondage and the Babylonian exile. These sad events in their past history were God's judgment upon a people who had failed to keep the law. There was no place for such faithlessness in the Qumran community.

Whereas God had once summoned all Israel to live in a covenanted relationship with him, the call must now go out on an individual basis. Any Jew who was willing to accept the sectarian interpretation of the law was eligible for membership. It meant separating himself from the Jerusalem priesthood and the religion practiced there. It meant the acceptance of communal life with all the rigors involved therein; but since there was no hope for salvation for those who rejected the sectarian interpretation of the covenant, it behooved the individual to consider seriously the call to sectarian living.

To make sure no member lapsed into faithlessness, the sectarians held an annual review. At this review, which may have come in the spring during the Jewish Festival of Weeks, the life of each member was examined for any possible faults or defects. The faithful rededicated themselves to the covenant and reaffirmed their faith in the truth of God made known to them through their Teacher of Righteousness. If it became known that any member had so much as associated with a banished member, the offender would be banished. The purity of the elect had to be preserved if God's covenant with this remnant was to be kept intact.

What Was the Sectarian View of Man?

Millar Burrows says that there is nothing more distinctive in Qumran theology than the doctrine of man and sin. Other scholars might prefer to single out the doctrine of the two spirits, the expectation of two messiahs, or the strong emphasis upon the sovereignty of God as being the most distinctive feature of Qumran theology, but there can certainly be no doubt that the sectarians took a dim view of man. Reading some of the Thanksgiving Psalms causes one to remember that precocious maker of rhymes, Isaac Watts, who at the age of seven wrote,

> I am a vile polluted lump of earth;
> So I've continued ever since my birth.

Actually, young Watts seems to have been more pessimistic about human nature than were the sectarians, but one of the Thanksgiving Psalms does refer to man as a sinner from the womb, fashioned from clay and continuing in his guilt to his old age. The first psalm in the Thanksgiving scroll is even more critical of man when it describes him as a source of pollution and a furnace of iniquity.

There is, however, no doctrine of original sin in the Thanksgiving Psalms. There is no suggestion that Adam's disobedience was the cause of man's sin. Neither do we find here the idea that flesh as such is *essentially* evil. Man is *actually* a sinner and in need of God's grace, and if he does not receive the spirit of truth and light from God, there is no hope that he can please God.

In the eighth psalm of our Bible, the poet considers the majesty of the heavens, the moon and the stars, and observes that though man is insignificant, yet God has conferred upon him the dignity of dominion within the created order. Even this guarded optimism is absent in the Thanksgiving Psalms.

It should be remembered, however, that man's situation is far from hopeless. The Manual of Discipline tells us that God created man to have dominion over the world. To this end, God endowed some men with the spirit of truth so that they would persevere in their obedience to the law. They would undoubtedly be attacked by the Angel of Darkness, but the God of Israel and his Angel of Truth would come to the defense of those whom God had elected. God would show mercy and steadfast love to those whom he had chosen.

Did the Sectarians Expect a Future Life?

The attitude of the sectarians toward the future life is ambiguous. We cannot be sure whether they contemplated any kind of future life, and if they did, we do not know whether they thought of this future life in terms of a resurrection from the sleep of death or in terms of the immortality of the soul.

In the eleventh column of the Thanksgiving scroll (to cite but one example), some scholars have found an implicit reference to a resurrection. It is stated in this particular text that, for the sake of God's glory, man has been cleansed from his transgression so that he can share the common lot of the angels, or holy ones. Those scholars who find here a reference to resurrection think that the poet was looking beyond the grave to the time when the righteous dead would be raised to share the lot of the angels. The text, however, is ambiguous. There is certainly no clear reference either to the immortality of the soul or to the resurrection of a dead man. On the contrary, it

104

may be that the sectarians in general, and this poet in particular, believed that righteous men who were still alive were already sharing with the angels a new and higher order of existence. Perhaps the sectarians thought of the holy ones as already present with them in their life at Qumran.

Menahem Mansoor of the University of Wisconsin thinks that he finds a reference to a resurrection in the sixth column of the Thanksgiving scroll. There is in this column an allusion to the raising of the flag or ensign by those who "lie in the dust." Mansoor points out that in one of the very few passages in the Old Testament where there is an actual reference to a resurrection (Isa. 26:19), the phrase "dwellers in the dust" clearly refers to the dead, as it does several times in the book of Job. Mansoor's interpretation is possible, but it is equally possible that the poet had in mind the final, futile rebellion of faithless and unrighteous men who, though alive, could still be described as those who "lie in the dust."

If it could be proved that the sectarians expected their dead Teacher of Righteousness to return in the new age, then there would be evidence that they did look forward to a future life. Or, if it could be shown that they expected the dead to be raised for a final judgment, this would be enlightening. Or again, if the occasional references in some of the Thanksgiving Psalms to a participation in things eternal could be construed as obvious references to a state of existence beyond the grave, a belief in either immortality or resurrection could be postulated. Thus far, all such attempts to prove that the sectarians believed in a future life seem to involve at least as much inference and conjecture as actual evidence.

In spite of the fact that no certain evidence can be produced for a belief in future life among the sectarians, I am willing to guess that they probably did accept such a hope. Their use of Daniel and certain noncanonical literature which do contain references to a future life would at least acquaint them with the idea. There is also some evidence that these sectarians were at least cousins of the Pharisees, who did believe in the possibility of a resurrection. Their vivid sense of impending doom for the wicked may also suggest by contrast that the sectarians expected the sons of light to share the blessings of God in an age without end.

Finally, if these sectarians were members of the Essenic movement—as I think they were—it should be recalled that Josephus states that the Essenes gave up their souls willingly because they expected to receive them again. Josephus' phrasing of the belief in terms of immortality may simply have been an accommodation to Hellenized readers who thought of future life in such terms, but the fact remains that Josephus did think of the Essenes as holding a belief in a future life. Whether this sectarian belief is to be described as a resurrection from the sleep of death or as the immortality of the soul is a question that has been impossible to answer on the basis of the evidence now available.

What Was the Prevailing Mood Among the Sectarians?

The apocalyptic mood prevailed among the sectarians. This is the mood encountered in the biblical books of Daniel and Revelation—a mood of war and rumors of war, a time of severe judgment for wicked men, a time of cosmic conflict and upheaval which must precede the new age. This mood is often prominent during periods of crisis. Thus, Daniel was written around 165 B.C., when devout Jews were being martyred because they remained faithful to the law. Likewise, the book of Revelation was written around A.D. 95, when Domitian's decree threatened the lives of the Christians. The strong note of conflict obvious in these books arose from the actual persecution and opposition each writer experienced in his own time.

This same mood can be felt in reading some of the literature from Qumran. The times were waxing late, and God's people were opposed by wicked men. Both heaven and earth were disturbed by the conflict between the forces of darkness and the forces of light. Even the angelic forces were taking up their weapons for the final war. Man was completely inadequate for such a moment, but fortunately God himself would fight for the right and the war would be won. The final judgment of the wicked would soon come and the sons of light would be exalted.

Meantime, the children of light could do their part by being obedient to the law God had given them. There must be no compromise with those who failed to obey the revealed will of God. The sectarians believed that the prophecies of olden times were being fulfilled in their midst. Their own Teacher of Righteousness had received special insight so that he and the members of the sect understood correctly the hidden meaning of the law and the prophets. The knowledge of God declared in his creative acts was being revealed in a mysterious and marvelous manner to the sectarians for their salvation. They had separated themselves from the wicked people of the world and were prepared to suffer whatever hardship might come, because they alone were God's elect and the final victory belonged to them.

VII

Jesus of Nazareth and the Teacher of Righteousness

Do the Dead Sea Scrolls Disprove the Uniqueness of Jesus?

IN HIS FIRST BOOK ON THE SUBJECT OF THE DEAD SEA SCROLLS, Dupont-Sommer, the French Orientalist, compared Jesus of Nazareth and the Teacher of Righteousness in the following words:

The Galilean Master, as He is presented to us in the writings of the New Testament, appears in many respects as an astonishing reincarnation of the Master of Justice. Like the latter he preached penitence, poverty, humility, love of one's neighbor, chastity. Like him, He prescribed the observance of the Law of Moses, the whole Law, but the Law finished and perfected, thanks to His own revelations. Like him He was the Elect and the Messiah of God, the Messiah redeemer of the world. Like him He was the object of the hostility of the priests, the party of the Sadducees. Like him He was condemned and put to death. Like him He pronounced judgment on Jerusalem, which was taken and destroyed by the Romans for having put Him to death. Like Him, at the end of time, He will be the supreme judge. Like him He founded a Church whose adherents fervently awaited His glorious return.[1]

When Wilson wrote his report on the scrolls, he quoted these words from Dupont-Sommer with some approval and hinted

---

[1] A. Dupont-Sommer, *The Dead Sea Scrolls*, p. 99.

that the uncommitted students of the subject would soon discover that Jesus was not unique in every respect. Suggestions such as these raised questions in the minds of readers about the originality of Jesus of Nazareth.

Only a moment of reflection will suffice to remind the reader that his answer to the above question will depend somewhat on his view of Jesus. In other words, he must first answer the question which the New Testament attributes to Jesus when he asks his disciples, "Who do you say that I am?"

I once knew a radiant and devout Christian lady who affirmed, with warmth and feeling, that for her Christ was a living presence in her life. She enjoyed, so she claimed, the knowledge that Christ was a spiritual power within her own heart. Her beliefs about Jesus were relatively few and straightforward. He was the Son of God, born of the Virgin, who lived and died on the cross so that sinful man could be saved. Being guiltless and sinless, Christ paid the debt for her sin, which she incurred as a descendant of Adam. Now that God's justice had been satisfied by Christ's sacrifice, the gates of heaven were opened to all who "knew Jesus Christ as their personal savior." As far as she was concerned, she was certain that God had raised Jesus from the dead and that he ruled in heaven with God, as well as on earth in her heart and in the lives of like-minded Christians.

The reader will certainly be aware of a second and very large group of Christians who tend to think of Jesus in quite different terms from those described above. For them Jesus may have been a noble teacher, a prophet with moral sensitivity, and a man of courage who believed in God. They may see Jesus as a new Socrates willing to die rather than compromise a principle. He was a Jewish leader with a magnetic personality who attracted crowds because of his able use of the parable and because, in a few instances, his powerful personality actually overcame the fears of sick people in such a way that they were cured emotionally, and hence physically. Basically, his ideas and teachings came from Judaism, but with a few subtle refinements which distinguished the Galilean from earlier teachers and prophets.

These Christians would deny the Virgin Birth and the Resurrection. Indeed, they would deny all supernatural dimensions in religion. Whatever is given in life will determine what shall be. Sociological, psychological, and economic factors influence greatly, and perhaps even determine, the direction and the degree of evolution in religious insights. They would not care to deny the genius and inspiration of Jesus, but they would suggest that other religious leaders have had similar gifts, and they would always want to compare Jesus' ideas with those of these others in an attempt to decide which religious leader is superior.

There is a third group of Christians who insist that the biblical faith is more than intellectual assent to a proposition, and even more than a new system of ideas or teachings. This third group puts emphasis on events in history. The Exodus and the Resurrection would be two such events. They suggest that biblical history is actually a story of God's saving and redeeming activity. God chose the Hebrew people, delivered them from Egypt, entered into a covenant with them and gave them law for their guidance. God's purpose in all this activity was to lead sinful and presumptuous man back to obedience and a renewed fellowship between God and his people. In the birth, life, death, and resurrection of Christ we have another event in which God has once more chosen mankind and entered as fully into mankind's history as it is possible for God to do. Incarnate in Christ, this God of suffering and holy love was buffeted by the evils in the world, but in the crucial moment of man's history his sovereign love emerged victorious and raised Jesus from the dead. As Paul puts it, "God shows his love for us in that while we were yet sinners Christ died for us." (Rom. 5:8.)

The heart of this interpretation of Christianity is the free and sovereign God who reveals himself to men in the events of history—especially the Christ event, which includes the birth, life, teaching and preaching career, suffering, death, and resurrection of Jesus. Christianity is not simply a higher level in the gradual evolution of moral and religious ideas. Christianity is the confrontation of men by God in Christ, an event which is not simply past history from the human point of view, but an event which still continues in the life of the church over which the risen Christ rules.

Such brief sketches of Christologies (doctrines of Christ) are certainly inadequate, and perhaps even confusing, but one thing should be clear. When we raise the question of the uniqueness of Jesus we must first consider the New Testament witness to Jesus and then make up our minds what our own view of him is. If we think of him as a superb teacher of morality with a sensitive social consciousness, we shall want to see whether the Teacher of Righteousness manifested similar qualities. If we think of Jesus as the unique Son of God whose life, death, and resurrection revealed the saving love of God, we shall turn to the Teacher of Righteousness with this criterion in mind as we make our comparison. If we stress continuity and evolution in history rather than discontinuity and revolution, this conviction will inevitably enter into any comparisons we make between the Teacher of Righteousness and Jesus of Nazareth.

Are There Differences Between Jesus and the Teacher of Righteousness?

From the point of view of the New Testament authors, there are many important differences between Jesus and the Teacher of Righteousness, as this latter figure is revealed in the literature from Qumran. For instance, the New Testament is thoroughly permeated by the conviction that God has raised Jesus from the dead. Peter affirms belief in the Resurrection when he delivers his address on the day of Pentecost. He says that God has "loosed the pangs of death" and that Jesus is assuredly Lord and Christ.

Paul gives us the earliest written record of the Resurrection in his first letter to the Corinthians. In this letter, he describes as of "first importance" the fact that Christ has died for our sins and has now been raised from the dead. The Resurrection is so important to Paul that he says his preaching is in vain if Christ has not been raised. For Paul, faith lacks a foundation if Christ does not live. It is the personal knowledge of the living Christ within his own life which has transformed Paul's personality. He is, as the Scottish professor James Stewart puts it, a new man in Christ. Paul is convinced that the Resurrection is both an objective fact of history and a subjective fact for him and for all believers.

Similar testimony can be found from the beginning to the end of the New Testament. The Gospels tell of an empty tomb and of the appearances of Christ to men in Galilee and in Judea. In all these accounts, there may be variations in detail, but one thing is clear: A dead man has been raised. Jesus lives! This is the faith which permeates the embryo of the church. This is the faith which produced Stephen and the other martyrs. This is the faith which we meet in the book of Revelation as Christians stand firm before the arrogance and pretensions of Rome. Some Christian theologians maintain that apart from the Resurrection there would be no faith, no church, and no Christianity.

I realize these are strong affirmations, and many people who want to consider themselves Christians will demur on the grounds that Jesus himself did not advocate such a faith but rather taught love for God and for man in the hope that men would soon learn to co-operate and build God's kingdom on earth. Be that as it may, no one can deny that the belief in the Resurrection is extremely important, if not decisive, for the New Testament authors.

The mood of the Qumran literature differs radically from that of the New Testament in regard to this belief in the Resurrection. It can be stated categorically that there is not a single text in all the Qumran scrolls which says that the Teacher of Righteousness has been raised from the dead. Even Allegro, who has done much to popularize the idea that the sectarians expected the crucified Teacher of Righteousness to return, does not care to argue for the view that the Qumran literature teaches the special resurrection of the Teacher of Righteousness as an accomplished fact. He merely suggests that the sectarians expected their Teacher to share in a general resurrection and return as the priestly Messiah.

At this point some words of caution are necessary for the unwary lay reader. Even if we grant for the moment that Allegro may be correct in his conjecture that the sectarians expected the Teacher of Righteousness to return, the difference between the fact of Jesus' resurrection, which shapes the entire mood of the early Christians, and what at the most is only a hope for a general resurrection among the sectarians should be carefully considered. In the New Testament, Peter, Paul, and the gospel writers tell us that God *has* raised Christ from the dead. God has acted in history to do an unusual deed. He has quite unexpectedly raised just one man from the dead. This is an individual's resurrection, not a hoped-for general resurrection such as the one Allegro thinks the sectarians had in mind.

Aside from the Resurrection, Are There Additional Differences?

There certainly are! From the stories of Jesus' birth to the interpretations of his death these differences come in rapid succession. At least two of the Gospels contain the stories of the Virgin Birth. Jesus did not have a male parent, but was, as the creed affirms it, "conceived by the Holy Ghost and born of the Virgin Mary." Magi of the East and shepherds of the field recognized this child's majesty and came to Bethlehem to worship. Whatever these stories may signify, the followers of the Teacher of Righteousness did not tell comparable stories about their leader. There is never any suggestion in the Dead Sea Scrolls of a miraculous birth for the Teacher of Righteousness.

The story of Jesus begins even earlier in the Fourth Gospel with the teaching of the pre-existence of Christ. In this Gospel we read that "In the beginning was the Word, and the Word was with God, and the Word was God," and in a later verse we read that this Word became flesh. The apostle Paul may have had a similar thought in mind when he wrote to the Christians of Philippi, urging them to adopt the same attitude as Christ, "who, though he was in the form of God, did not count equality with God a thing to be grasped, but emptied himself, taking the form of a servant, being born in the likeness of men" (Phil. 2:5-7).

There is nothing in the Dead Sea Scrolls about the pre-existence of the Teacher of Righteousness. Dupont-Sommer had originally thought that a reference in the Habakkuk Commentary to someone suffering in "his body of flesh," was "without doubt" a reference to the pre-existent, divine Teacher of Righteousness who became incarnate and suffered and died in his body of flesh.[2] The fact is that the text of the Habakkuk Commentary is missing at the very point where the subject of this suffering would normally be expressed. Though Dupont-Sommer was "without doubt" that his conjecture was correct, other scholars were not convinced, and suggested that this passage might well refer to the suffering of the Wicked Priest rather than to the suffering of the Teacher of Righteousness. Today, even Dupont-Sommer has modified his earlier hypothesis.

In the preceding quotation from the Fourth Gospel, contact was made with another doctrine which is not found in the Dead Sea Scrolls. This is the doctrine of Incarnation, or the doctrine that in some sense God became flesh in Christ. This doctrine, like that of the Resurrection, is so integral to Christianity that to remove it is to proclaim a religion not quite like that espoused by the New Testament. Walter Marshall Horton

[2] A. Dupont-Sommer, *The Dead Sea Scrolls*, p. 34.

of Oberlin College once put this doctrine into verse simple enough for all to understand. The verse went something like this:

> Willie, Willie, get your drum;
> Ta ta ra, ta ta ra, ta ta ra.
> God and man have now become
> More at one than fife and drum;
> Ta ta ra, ta ta ra, ta ta ra.

And I remember another famous American theologian who visited our campus and said that if he had to reduce his understanding of Christianity to one word, it would probably be "Incarnationism."

This is not the place to enter into a detailed analysis of the meaning of this New Testament teaching, but in short the New Testament authors seem to be saying that the power, the authority, and the holy love of God were so mediated through Christ that sins were forgiven, diseases were healed, the Kingdom was present, and even death was overcome. Jesus may not have been far from making some such claim for himself when he said, "But if it is by the finger of God that I cast out demons, then the kingdom of God has come upon you" (Luke 11:20). Jesus seemed to speak and act with an authority born of his sense of the immediate and complete claim of God upon his life.

Of all this, there is no evidence in the Dead Sea Scrolls. It is true that the Teacher of Righteousness was regarded as having been endowed with special knowledge which permitted him to interpret the law and the prophets correctly; but in the case of Jesus, God's new word was not so much a new written or spoken interpretation of the existing law and the prophets as it was a new word of God's self-revelation in the life, death, and resurrection of a particular man. I think it was Harry Emerson Fosdick who once said that the disciples looked at Jesus until

115

their gaze pierced the outer shell of the man and saw something that was unique in man's history. They saw God there. The Dead Sea Scrolls do not make a similar claim for the Teacher of Righteousness.

Was the Teacher of Righteousness Regarded as a Savior?

No, he was not. There is evidence that he suffered as a martyr, but there is no evidence that his followers ever regarded him as one whose death saved men from either sin or death. The death of the Teacher of Righteousness receives so little attention in the Dead Sea Scrolls that it is not known how he died. Milik is certainly correct in saying that no text in the Dead Sea Scrolls clearly affirms a violent death for the Teacher. The Damascus Document mentions the "gathering in" of the Teacher, but this may be no more than a reference to the natural death of a man.

This scant attention to the death of the Teacher of Righteousness should be contrasted with the emphasis placed on the death of Christ by the New Testament writers. At least one third of Mark's Gospel is concerned directly with the last week in Jesus' life. The story of Jesus' trial, scourging, bearing of the cross to Golgotha, and crucifixion are so well known that most Christians can recount it without too much difficulty. One need only remember the millions of Roman Catholics who speak of the sacrifice of the Mass to realize how important the death of Christ is to the church.

When early Christians reflected upon the meaning of Christ's death, they associated it with the love of God. To paraphrase a well-known verse of scripture, they believed that God loved the world so much that he gave of himself in an only Son so that believers might have life eternal. Paul has already been quoted to show that he saw God's love for sinners in the death of Christ, and here might be added another quotation from him which says, "God was in Christ reconciling the world to himself" (II Cor. 5:19). For Paul, there is nothing in all God's creation that can separate man from the love of God which was in Christ Jesus his Lord. This love defeats the powers and principalities which separate men from God, and removes the sting from death itself. Christ is Savior in the New Testament, but because of the incarnation theme, it follows immediately that God is Savior. The Dead Sea Scrolls make no such claims for the Teacher of Righteousness.

It is sometimes argued that faith in the Teacher of Righteousness saves, just as faith in Christ saves. This suggestion is based on the text of the Habakkuk Commentary, which says that God will deliver from the house of judgment those who labor and have "faith in the Teacher of Righteousness." Those who argue for this position point out that in Paul's letters the apostle also encourages faith and says that men are justified by faith. Paul, so they say, even says that it is a faith in Christ which saves.

The danger of this type of comparison is that it may too easily identify basic concepts on the basis of mere verbal similarity. It is not really correct to say that Paul and the author of the Habakkuk Commentary are in agreement simply because both of them say something about the efficacy of faith in their respective leaders. What does faith mean for the author of this Dead Sea Scroll? And what does Paul mean when he speaks about faith in Christ? Each of these questions could very easily become dissertation topics, but the general conclusions which we need here can be summarized briefly.

When the author of the Habakkuk Commentary mentions faith in the Teacher of Righteousness, he seems to have in mind a loyalty to the Teacher that reveals itself in the sectarian's willingness to keep the law as it is interpreted by the Teacher and the Qumran community. If they trust the Teacher's leadership and abide by the rules he has established, God will deliver them from the judgment which will soon come in fury against the sons of darkness.

Faith, for Paul, means different things. It may simply be a reference to the religion of Jesus' followers, or perhaps a confidence in the outcome of an action whose results cannot be known for certain. But when Paul speaks of faith in Christ, he may well introduce a mystical element that cannot be found in the Habakkuk Commentary. It has been estimated that Paul uses the expression "in Christ" as many as sixty times in his letters. To understand Paul's meaning, we must not forget that for him Christ is a living presence. To be in Christ is more than to have confidence in a man; it is to feel the Spirit of Christ within in such a way that the old, natural man gives way to the new, spiritual man. Faith in Christ is life with the risen Lord and the assurance that the Spirit is the pledge and guarantee of a salvation and deliverance which is both present fact and future expectation.

There may be mystical overtones in the sectarian religion. Many students of the Dead Sea Scrolls think that there are, but there is no evidence that the sectarians have a mystical union with a risen Savior.

Did Jesus Ever Live at Qumran?

Günther Bornkamm, professor of New Testament at the University of Heidelberg, has made a careful and scholarly study of the life of Jesus and its impact upon first-century believers. It is Bornkamm's conclusion that there is no evidence in the Gospels that Jesus ever lived at Qumran or had any immediate contact with the Essenes. He admits there may be some similarities between the theological views of the Essenes and the theology of the original Palestinian church and adds that the communal discipline of this church may in some respects be similar to that which prevailed among the Essenes, but he finds no evidence for believing that Jesus ever went to Qumran and lived with the sectarians.

At least one writer on the subject of the scrolls, the Rev. Dr.

Charles Francis Potter, disagrees with Bornkamm.[3] Potter is convinced that the Dead Sea Scrolls "have given us the answer at last" to the question, "Where did Jesus live and what was he doing between the age of twelve and the age of thirty?" Potter claims that it is becoming increasingly apparent that Jesus spent this period of his life at Qumran studying sectarian doctrines.

The evidence, however, favors Bornkamm's conclusion. The differences between Jesus' way of living and that of the Teacher of Righteousness are so important as to raise serious doubt whether Jesus ever shared the Qumran way of life. Jesus mingled with publicans, tax collectors, the lame, the blind, the dumb, and the sinners. He went to Jerusalem to sacrifice at the Temple. Whereas Jesus respected the law and often urged men to follow its statutes, his own attitude toward the sabbath was so free as to incur the displeasure of the Pharisees when he healed on the sabbath and permitted his disciples to pluck ears of grain. Like the prophet Nathan, who convicted David by a well-told parable, Jesus also employed lively metaphor, pointed parable, and radical contrasts to drive home his teaching. The sheep of the field, the birds of the air, the salt of the earth, the wedding feast, and even the fish of the sea were examples cited by Jesus to teach men about the kingdom of God.

In contrast, the Teacher of Righteousness was a priest who lived a secluded life in the wilderness of Judea. The discipline within his community was rigorous, to say the least. Outsiders were shunned and there was no room for the physically handicapped in Qumran. The Teacher of Righteousness and his followers were opposed to the Jerusalem priesthood and much preferred their ritual and festivals celebrated according to their own calendar. It is not certain whether the sectarians offered sacrifice at Qumran, but it is known that they refused to co-operate with the priests at the Temple.

[3] See the back cover of Potter's book, *The Lost Years of Jesus Revealed* (Greenwich, Conn.: Fawcett Publications, Inc., 1958).

The rules of sabbath observance are laid out in some detail in the Damascus Document. Business transactions, frivolous talk, and extended walks outside the community are strictly forbidden. Normative Judaism would permit a man to walk about three thousand feet outside his city before it was counted a sabbath infraction, but in the strict life of the sectarians this limit was reduced to about fifteen hundred feet.

Jesus says, "What man of you, if he has one sheep and it falls into a pit on the sabbath, will not lay hold of it and lift it out?" (Matt. 12:11.) We could now answer Jesus and say, "the sectarians." One of the passages in the Damascus Document forbids the sectarians to rescue a baby animal from a cistern or a pit if it has been dropped there in birth on the sabbath. Indeed, this same Damascus Document says that neither ladder nor rope nor any other instrument is to be used to rescue a man who has fallen into the water on the sabbath. The latter attitude seems so inconsistent with that of normative Judaism that Gaster, the Jewish scholar, emends the text in order to make it yield the opposite meaning. While Gaster's instinct may be correct here, it is also just possible that these sectarians were unusually rigorous in their keeping of the sabbath commandment.

Are There Similarities Between Jesus and the Teacher of Righteousness?

The less traditional Christians may object to much that has been stated heretofore in this chapter on the grounds that the doctrines of the Virgin Birth, the Incarnation, the Resurrection, and pre-existence represent the theological positions of Paul and the Gospel writers rather than the clear, straightforward, and humble preaching of Jesus. Jesus did not want to be identified with God, but rather wished to acknowledge his absolute dependence upon God. He did not claim to be the Messiah; he was much more interested in the poor and the downtrodden. His mission in life was to help the sick, condemn the arrogant

120

and self-righteous, teach the importance of inner motivations, and encourage the growth of the spiritual life. Jesus wanted social justice. He was against hypocrisy in religion. These are the *facts* of Jesus' life as opposed to the theological affirmations made about him by his later followers. And the facts of Jesus' life, rather than the faith about him, should be used as a basis for comparison with the Teacher of Righteousness.

Appealing as this line of thought seems to be at first glance, it does raise some questions which the reader should consider before continuing his comparison of Jesus and the Teacher of Righteousness. Does the New Testament really distinguish sharply between the event of Jesus' historic existence and the interpretation of this event by the believing community? Is it actually possible to read the New Testament in such a discerning manner that one can see both a Jesus of history and another figure who can be described as the Christ of faith? Perhaps *the fact* from the New Testament point of view includes both the *fact* of Jesus' life and the *interpretation* of that fact. Perhaps it is not the intention of the New Testament writers to provide a detailed biographical account of Jesus, but rather an interpretation of the meaning of Jesus' life as felt by men who believed that God had raised Jesus from the dead.

If these questions represent an actual truth about the New Testament, it may be exceedingly difficult to find in its pages a photographic facsimile of a teacher, Jesus, whose instruction can be compared with that of the leader of the Qumran sectarians. If there is, instead, a portrait of Jesus which includes such themes as Incarnation and Resurrection, it may be arbitrary to see Jesus' significance only in terms of his teachings and moral insights, though these are indeed important.

These questions and qualifications notwithstanding, we need not abandon the task of comparing some of Jesus' teachings with those of the Teacher of Righteousness as seen in some of the Dead Sea Scrolls. The Gospel According to Mark states that Jesus began his ministry by proclaiming, "The time is fulfilled, and the kingdom of God is at hand; repent, and believe in the gospel" (Mark 1:15). While the exact terminology of this verse may be influenced by the early church, there is good reason to believe that Jesus saw his own life as a bridge connecting the old and the new ages. The kingdom of God had not arrived in full, but the signs of its imminent coming were unmistakable. God's appointed time had come upon the people. There was still time for repentance, but the time was so short that there was an extreme urgency to repent quickly. The judgment of God would come unexpectedly like a thief in the night and catch the unwary unprepared.

We have already seen that the Teacher of Righteousness and the sectarians saw themselves to be living at the end of days. The time foretold by the prophets was being fulfilled in the life of the sect. There was still time for men to repent and join the community at Qumran, but the appointed time of God's judgment was hastening to its wrathful end. The opposing armies for the final great conflict were being organized. The battle lines were being drawn up and the strategy was being planned. Men must separate themselves from the heretical priesthood and worship at Jerusalem and accept the sectarian way of life; otherwise, they would be judged by God, who had determined to exterminate the sons of darkness.

The details differ, but both Jesus and the Teacher of Righteousness shared a similar timetable. The appointed time of God had come, and judgment hovered over them like an impending doom. It was, however, a timetable well known to the apocalyptic thinkers of Judaism, so we must be careful not to overwork this similarity in an attempt to prove a relationship between Jesus and the Teacher of Righteousness.

Other possible points of contact between the Teacher of Righteousness and Jesus may be found in their respective attitudes toward material possessions, the meek and the poor, the proper procedure for the rebuke of an erring brother, and possibly even in their common understanding that ritual washing availed nothing if not preceded by repentance. It is also possible that both men looked forward to the coming of a messianic figure (s) , though in this matter it would be very helpful if it were known just how Jesus and the Teacher of Righteousness related their own missions to those of the expected Messiah or messiahs.

These similarities bring to mind qualifications and questions, however. Did Jesus, who lived among the ordinary people of the land, renounce property in the same way that the Teacher of Righteousness did? When Jesus spoke of the poor, was he speaking of the poor at Qumran or of the poor in spirit who were humble and self-effacing? Did Jesus put even more stress upon inner motivation than did the Teacher of Righteousness, whose community had set up strict punishments for those who failed to abide by the rules of the sectarian organization? Did the aura of authority which accompanied Jesus' actions indicate his sense of an immediate relationship to God that we cannot find in the Teacher of Righteousness? These qualifications and questions are so important that great caution should be exercised when comparing Jesus and the Teacher of Righteousness.

Is Dupont-Sommer's Comparison of the Teacher and Jesus Valid?

The chapter began with a quotation from Dupont-Sommer comparing Jesus and the Teacher of Righteousness. In this quotation, Dupont-Sommer says that in many respects Jesus is an astonishing reincarnation of the Teacher of Righteousness. In a footnote, he makes it clear that he does not wish to deny the originality of Christianity or identify Jesus, who was a real historical personage, with the Teacher of Righteousness who died more than a half century before Jesus was born. But as Dupont-Sommer's most recent book shows, he still sees many interesting parallels between these two leaders of religious movements.[4]

[4] A. Dupont-Sommer, *Die Essenischen Schriften*, pp. 402 ff.

In a general way I can agree with Dupont-Sommer when he says that Christianity is grafted onto the tree of Judaism. Maybe I could even go further and say that Christianity is more than a graft (no pun intended). Christianity has its original roots firmly imbedded in the soil of Judaism. Jesus was a Jew. He spoke the language of Judaism, lived the life of Judaism, and worshiped with Judaism. The similarities between Jesus and Judaism are not inconsiderable, but it must be added that many of these similarities were already known before the Dead Sea Scrolls were found.

In the particulars, however, I must disagree with Dupont-Sommer. There is no compelling reason to believe that the Teacher of Righteousness was the "elect" of God; rather, the reference to the "elect" in the Habakkuk Commentary is probably to the sectarians who were members of the community, and not to the Teacher of Righteousness. Nor is it certain that either the Teacher or Jesus claimed to be a messiah. The weight of evidence seems to be definitely against such a thesis. It is clear that the New Testament writers make this claim for Jesus —more than can be said for the Qumran literature—but it is not certain that Jesus applied this designation to himself.

Dupont-Sommer suggests that both leaders are redeemers, but here I must object that the word "redeemer" has so many meanings in the life of Judaism and Christianity that there must first be some definitions before any meaningful equations between the Teacher and Jesus can be made. In one sense, the nearest kinsman of the biblical Ruth could have been a redeemer if he had saved Naomi and Ruth from economic embarrassment by buying the piece of land they were offering for sale. In another sense, God was redeemer when he delivered the Hebrew people from Egypt. In Christianity, the Christ-event has redemptive qualities because of God's activity in this event. Some would say that Christ is redeemer because his death and resurrection signaled the climactic defeat of both sin and death, thereby making possible a new union or at-one-ment between man and God.

It is difficult to see that the Teacher fits any of these descriptions. He did not redeem land and save kinsmen from economic pressures. He was not God who redeemed either from Egypt or from death. He was not the Incarnate One whose death and resurrection served as a redemption for sinful man. It may well be that the Teacher did mediate God's truths to the sectarians and help organize them for battle in such a way that they would be redeemed from the sons of darkness, but I think that an easy equation of the redemptive activities of the Teacher and Jesus is not possible.

If Jesus and the Teacher preached penitence, so did Jeremiah. If both leaders spoke out against wealth, so did Amos. If both recommended love of neighbor, so did the book of Leviticus. If both regarded chastity as a virtue, so did the Torah of Israel. If both men had trouble with the authorities in Jerusalem, so did Jeremiah. If both men pronounced judgment on Jerusalem, so did Micah and Ezekiel. And as for Dupont-Sommer's contention that the Teacher was put to death and was expected to return at the end of time as a supreme judge, the Dead Sea Scrolls tell nothing about the exact manner of the Teacher's death and leave us in doubt as to whether the sectarians really looked forward to the glorious return of their dead leader.

In his latest book, Dupont-Sommer maintains that both the Teacher and Jesus saw themselves as the Suffering Servant predicted by Second Isaiah. From the standpoint of Christian faith we might like to say that Jesus did see his life as a fulfillment of the role of the Suffering Servant, but we must admit that New Testament scholars have long denied that Jesus ever claimed to play such a role.

It begins to become evident, therefore, how tenuous many of Dupont-Sommer's conclusions really are. Where there are genuine parallels between the Teacher and Jesus, similar parallels can be drawn from the Law and the Prophets. In other instances, conjectures that cannot be proved from the actual texts of the Dead Sea Scrolls are offered to make the Teacher's death and supposed reappearance parallel Jesus' death and resurrection. In light of these facts, let us move cautiously before drawing connecting lines between the Teacher of Righteousness and Jesus of Nazareth.

VIII

The Scrolls and the New Testament

Do the Scrolls Shed New Light on the New Testament?

THE DEAD SEA SCROLLS ARE LIKELY TO SHED SOME NEW LIGHT on the New Testament. If nothing else, the Dead Sea Scrolls will help us understand the beliefs, practices, and aspirations of a group of Jews who lived near the Dead Sea while Jesus was engaged in his active ministry. Since it is universally granted that Jesus was a Jew, it is important to know as much as possible about the Jews who were Jesus' contemporaries. To understand thoroughly the thoughts and actions of the Jews who lived in Palestine during the first century before Christ and the first century after Christ, is to know the atmosphere in which Jesus "lived and moved and had his being." It is to come into contact with thought forms and patterns which have almost certainly affected the moral and intellectual life of the Galilean.

If the Aramaic of the Genesis Apocryphon enables us to better understand the dialect used by the Palestinian Jews in the days of Jesus, we may be in a better position to judge what kind of Aramaic expressions of Jesus are now reflected in our Greek New Testament. If we learn more about the sectarian hopes for the coming of the messiahs and their expectations for final judgment, we may be able to grasp more adequately similar subjects when we meet them in the teachings of Jesus. If the scrolls present to us a group of sectarians who had voluntarily separated themselves from the Jerusalem priesthood, we may begin to feel the tensions within Judaism during Jesus' ministry.

To admit that Jesus was in many respects a child of his age does not necessarily threaten or compromise the claims of traditional Christianity that Jesus was the Incarnate Son of God who is the Risen Savior of all mankind. Christianity has always affirmed both the humanity and the divinity of its Lord; indeed, the first heresy within the church was the heresy which denied true humanity to Christ. If humanity means what it normally means, there is ample reason for believing that Jesus' teachings and his religious practices were influenced by those who lived near him in Palestine.

More specifically, it is at least conceivable that the common meal of the Qumran community may have influenced the procedure at the Last Supper. Or there may be a relationship between the use of water for ritual purposes at Qumran and Jesus' baptism by John the Baptist. It may even be possible that the organizational pattern of the Qumran community is found again in the early Christian church. And some of the language of the New Testament may have been derived from the sectarian language. These are some of the possibilities which we shall want to examine in this chapter on the scrolls and the New Testament.

Is Christian Baptism Derived from a Qumran Practice?

As in the case of Jesus and the Teacher of Righteousness, where it was necessary to explain possible views of Jesus' significance for the Christian faith before attempting to compare him with the sectarian Teacher of Righteousness, so here it must be pointed out that baptism means different things to different Christians, even though most of these Christians claim New Testament authority for their respective interpretations of this sacrament.

Most Christians regard baptism as a sacrament, and hence believe that in some way the grace of God is mediated through the water and words which normally accompany this Christian rite. Roman Catholics state clearly and unequivocally that the unbaptized soul cannot go to heaven because it still bears the taint of original sin. They believe that this is the only one of the seven sacraments that can free the soul from original sin, and therefore urge that it be administered to a baby as soon as possible.

Either a Protestant or a Catholic, lay or clerical, can administer the sacrament of baptism provided he uses water and baptizes in the name of the Father, Son, and Holy Ghost. The administering agent need not be a priest if it is really his intention to perform a Christian baptism. Once the sacrament has been validly given, it can never be repeated. It marks the recipient with an indelible character. By the very reason that the act or sacrament has been given, grace has been imparted and Original Sin removed from the infant's soul. So teaches the Roman Catholic Church.

Protestant interpretations of baptism vary, some Protestants even refusing to call it a sacrament. It may be regarded simply as a commemorative act which reminds the participant of Jesus' baptism and encourages him to lead the kind of selfless life Jesus exhibited. In this case, the value of the sacrament resides primarily in whatever good psychological effect it may have upon the individual and the community where it is administered. If the person being baptized does not really commit himself to the Christian faith at the moment of baptism, no grace will be imparted. The sacrament becomes dependent upon the inner disposition of the participant. Grace does not come automatically when the water is used and the Trinitarian formula is pronounced. The efficacy of the sacrament is almost entirely dependent upon the attitude of the recipient.

Other Protestants believe that baptism is a "washing of regeneration" (Tit. 3:5) which actually creates a new spiritual life and brings with it a promise of redemption from sin and death. This regeneration is accomplished by God's free gift of

129

the Holy Spirit which comes to the church and the individual through the risen Lord. In this baptism, the free grace of God acts to count the unrighteous man righteous while he is yet a sinner and at the same time becomes the effective agent of rebirth within a person's life. Salvation becomes a fact for the baptized individual, albeit a fact which cannot be fully realized in the present age.

With these possible interpretations of Christian baptism in mind, we can now consider whether or not the Christian rite is derived from the sectarian practice described in the Dead Sea Scrolls. The Manual of Discipline states that mere washing with water avails nothing if the person has not repented or turned away from his evil. Immediately, we remember that many Christians refuse to baptize infants because they believe that the baptized person must be an adult who is mature enough to recognize his past sin, repent of it, and willingly dedicate himself to the Christian faith. It would seem, therefore, that some Christians and sectarians agree that baptism loses its efficacy if it is not preceded by true repentance.

At this point, however, some qualifications that illustrate differences between Christians and sectarians must be introduced. First, there are literally millions of Christians who practice infant baptism, where repentance on the part of the recipient is not possible. At least some of these millions of Christians will insist that the sacrament bestows grace automatically when the sacrament is rightly administered. The sectarians, so far as we know, did not practice infant baptism, nor did they believe that their washing with water was a sacrament which imparted grace and an indelible character.

Secondly, repentance may not have meant quite the same thing for the sectarian that it now means for the Christian. For the sectarian, repentance meant a rejection of the Jerusalem priesthood and a commitment to abide by the law of Moses as it was interpreted by the sons of Zadok for the sectarian community. The Christian, on the other hand, may view repentance as a turning away from pride and hardness of heart, which rejects the forgiving and holy love of God revealed in the life, death, and resurrection of Christ.

A third possible difference between Christian baptism and the Qumran practice of washing with water involves the frequency of the act. Christian baptism is administered only once in a lifetime. While there is some uncertainty about it, there are some indications that the Qumran washings were repeated at regular intervals.

The fourth and decisive difference between Christian baptism and the ritual washing (s) of Qumran is the figure of Jesus. Christian baptism is performed in the name of the risen Christ. It symbolizes the immediate inclusion of the baptized person into the community whose ruler is the resurrected Lord. There is certainly nothing comparable to this among the sectarians.

It is also true that the sectarians did not think of their washing with water as an act which removed the taint of original sin. They believed that man was a sinner, and may even have agreed with one of our former colleagues who observed that man is fairly original in the way that he sins, but they certainly had no doctrine of original sin.

Briefly, then, my answer to the above question is this: Christian baptism may derive indirectly from the ritual washings of Judaism and even more directly from a Qumran practice, but Christian baptism as it is understood by the majority of Christians in the world today is much different from the sectarian practice.

Was John the Baptist Influenced by the Qumran Community?

There is no direct evidence that John was ever a member of the Qumran community. The fact that John lived in the wilderness, preached repentance, baptized in the Jordan, ate locusts and honey, wore rough garments of camel's hair and a leather girdle, does not prove that John was a member of the Qumran

131

community. There is considerable probability that John was aware of the sectarian way of life, and there is even a possibility that he might have lived at Qumran for a time, but we must be careful not to equate possibilities and probabilities with actualities.

For each of the seeming similarities between John the Baptist's life and teaching and that of the sectarians there can be listed an equally impressive difference. For instance: John's father was a Jerusalem priest who served at the Temple in Jerusalem. Would John have left his father and joined a group of sectarians who were utterly opposed to the Jerusalem priesthood? When we meet John in the New Testament, he is certainly not a member of the Qumran community, but a popular preacher of repentance who enjoys such a following that the chief priests, scribes, and elders are afraid to question his authority lest the multitudes who approve of John's work and preaching turn against them.

Unlike the sectarians, John offered membership in the kingdom of God to all men who repented. It was not necessary to be a member of the Qumran community in order to be saved. As Rowley notes, John's baptism was not an initiation into an organized community, but a preparation for a kingdom that was soon to come. To be sure, the sectarians also expected an imminent judgment, but there was an exclusiveness about their thinking that is not found in John's preaching.

There are many other differences between John and the sectarians. John did not demand long, probationary periods of those who wanted his baptism. Those who truly repented were eligible for baptism and immediate status as followers of John. Those who repented did not wash themselves, as was the custom among the sectarians, but rather permitted John to be the agent in the baptismal rite. John ate locusts and honey, wore camel's hair clothing, and a girdle made of leather whereas the sectarians may have eaten bread and one hot dish (exact contents unknown) and dressed in white garments. Some scholars have suggested that John's wilderness was none other than the very area of Qumran, but in light of these differences such an identification would seem somewhat hazardous.

There are, however, some interesting parallels between John and the sectarians. He did preach repentance. He did collect about himself a group of people who looked forward to the coming of the Messiah (not the two messiahs of the Qumran literature). He also believed that the judgment of God would soon fall like a devouring fire upon the wicked. His very choice of the wilderness rather than the towns as a setting for his ministry was reminiscent of the Qumran way of life. Like the sectarians, he interpreted his own mission as that of one who was "crying in the wilderness: Prepare the way of the Lord." And like them he may have seen himself as standing at the end of the old age heralding the imminent coming of the new age. People would have to repent quickly if they were to avoid the final judgment.

All that can be said in conclusion is that there may have been some relationship between John and Qumran. Perhaps both Jesus and John drew followers from the sectarian movement. The similarities of John's movement to that of the Qumran sectarians were such that converts to John's preaching would not have felt they were entering a completely alien territory. And the differences notwithstanding, it is even conceivable that John may have had some direct contacts with the Qumran community.

Does the Lord's Supper Evolve
from the Qumran Common Meal?

This is an extremely difficult question to answer because modern Christians are not agreed upon the interpretation of the New Testament accounts of the Lord's Supper. Roman Catholicism teaches the doctrine of transubstantiation. According to this doctrine, the very substance of the consecrated elements becomes the body and blood of Christ when the priest pronounces the words of institution. This sacrament originated with Jesus, who sat with his disciples for their last meal together and said of the bread, "This is my body," and of the wine, "This is my blood." Roman Catholics believe they are accepting the literal and obvious meaning of Jesus and the New Testament when they insist that the body and blood of Jesus are really present in this sacrament.

Lutherans, on the other hand, deny transubstantiation and are content to say that Christ is really present "in, with, and under" the consecrated elements. They agree that the Lord's Supper is a sacrament, but they reject the Roman Catholic view that Jesus actually transforms the substance of the bread and wine into his own body and blood. Lutherans believe in the Real Presence of Christ and stress the significance of this sacrament to the extent that some Lutherans practice closed Communion and exclude (in order to protect those people who may not be properly instructed as to the meaning of the sacrament) other Christians from their communion table.

Still other Protestants regard the Lord's Supper as a memorial of Jesus' crucifixion and death. They may or may not believe that Christ is spiritually present to be apprehended by faith, but they will certainly feel that they are participating in this sacrament to remember what Christ has done for them.

We see, therefore, that there are many different aspects to the Lord's Supper. Some Christians emphasize the sacrificial aspect and believe that in this sacrament the body and blood of Christ are presented to God as a sacrifice for the sins of the people. Other Christians emphasize the Communion aspect and teach that Christians commune with the living Lord who is spiritually present at the Lord's Table. Still others see this Christian rite as a time when all committed Christians should make a moral rededication of their lives. It is, of course, possible to hold all these views simultaneously, placing emphasis on that special aspect which seems most akin to the original intention of Jesus as he instituted this sacrament. But the very fact that this sacrament presents a major obstacle in any attempt at church union should be sufficient warning of the dangers of making simple and easy comparisons of the Lord's Supper and the common meal of Qumran.

The New Testament itself is at least partially responsible for these varying interpretations. It is impossible here to go into a detailed analysis of the problems presented to the interpreter by the New Testament text, but enough of these can be suggested to indicate to the reader why many competent scholars are cautious about viewing the Last Supper as the product of an evolutionary process which began with the common meal of Qumran.

First, was the Last Supper (if, indeed, it was a supper) actually a Passover meal? When Jesus' last meal is described in the Gospel According to Mark, no mention is made of unleavened bread, bitter herbs, lamb, or other food which is really distinctive of the Passover meal. Still, the authors of the Synoptic Gospels do seem to say that this last meal was a Passover, whereas the author of the Fourth Gospel states clearly that Jesus' last meal was eaten before the Passover. Which view is correct? Until this question can be answered, the exact relationship between Jesus' last meal and the Qumran common meal will remain uncertain.

A second problem in the interpretation of the New Testament account of the Lord's Supper is the injunction, supposedly of Jesus, to "Do this in remembrance of me." Apart from one questionable reference to this command in the Gospel According to Luke, we have only Paul's testimony. Did Jesus really urge his disciples to remember him, or is this a later addition to the story made by the church which thought it was an appropriate interpretation for devout followers of the Lord? On the basis of textual evidence alone, I am inclined to doubt the originality of this particular injunction. Moreover, I am not quite convinced that such an injunction is in keeping with

Jesus' humility, which is so obvious in other passages in the New Testament.

The relationship between the love feast (Jude 1:12) of early Christians and the celebration of the Lord's Supper is a third problem. Does the Lord's Supper grow out of the love feast or were they originally two separate rites? Were they both related to the common meals of the early church as these are described in Acts?

In modern Christendom, the Greek Orthodox Church makes a sharp distinction between Holy Communion and the agape, or love feast. I remember visiting a Greek church in Louisville and being approached after the liturgy had ended by a communicant who offered me a small portion of leavened bread. Being unfamiliar with this particular custom, I first thought I was being offered a portion of the consecrated elements and was about to refuse the bread because I was not a member of this particular communion and hence not eligible to receive Communion. The smile of the member plus his outstretched hand was accompanied by remarks to the effect that this was the bread of the love feast, unconsecrated and available to all who intend to live in Christian love and charity with their neighbors.

Such problems may seem unduly subtle to the lay reader, but as in the case of Jesus and the sacrament of baptism we must first know what the New Testament says and what we believe about these things before we can make comparisons of Christian practices and beliefs with Qumran practices and beliefs. With these problems and qualifications in mind, we can move on to the next question, which enables us to make a more detailed comparison of the Lord's Supper and the common meal of Qumran.

In What Respects Does the Lord's Supper Agree with and Differ from the Qumran Common Meal?

The Manual of Discipline from Qumran states that novices were excluded from participation in this meal. Only initiated members could partake of this food and drink. In this respect, it may be misleading to refer to the "common meal" of the sectarians. Rather, it was a special privilege reserved for those who had committed themselves to the interpretation of the law and the regulatory rules which prevailed among the sectarians. Conversely, an initiated member of the community was forbidden to eat food prepared by the wicked people who had rejected the sectarian faith and way of life.

We also learn from the Manual of Discipline that no food was to be eaten before it had been blessed by the priest. When all had been seated according to their rank in the community, the priest stretched forth his hand and offered a blessing over the first portion of bread and wine. Only after this grace had been offered could the sectarians commence their meal together.

Josephus describes a similar ceremony performed in the Essene Community. According to Josephus, these Essenes came in from their work, donned white garments, bathed in cold water, and then sat down for a meal of bread plus one hot dish. Eating before the priest offered his blessing was strictly forbidden. There was also a grace and a praising of God after the meal.

The Rule of the Congregation probably describes the same types of meals as described in the Manual of Discipline, but in this case it is described as a foreshadowing of the banquet which will take place in the messianic age when both messiahs are present. This meal becomes, therefore, a dramatic rehearsal or liturgical anticipation of the messianic banquet. According to the Rule of the Congregation, the food in this banquet will be blessed by both the priestly messiah and the royal messiah in turn. Then every man in the congregation, according to his rank, will bless the food before eating. Thus, it can be seen that the blessing of the bread and wine was standard procedure and that participation in the present meal of the community may have served to give expression to the sectarians' expectation that the messiahs of Aaron and Israel would soon stand among them.

The one other fact which should be remembered in connection with the common meal of the sectarians is the discovery in 1955 of almost forty deposits of animals' bones in the immediate vicinity of Qumran. It has already been suggested that these bones may represent the remains of meat eaten on the occasion of the annual review which may have come in the spring of the year when the sectarians celebrated the Festival of Weeks. Such careful burials as these cause speculation as to whether special sanctity was attached to the meals during which this meat was consumed.

With these facts about the sectarian meal in mind, a comparison of this meal with the Lord's Supper can now be made. Clarence Craig, a former professor of New Testament at Oberlin, Yale, and Drew, says that Paul's description of the Lord's Supper found in his letter to the Corinthian Christians is the "clearest picture of a Eucharistic celebration which we possess from the first century"; so we shall begin our comparison of the two meals with Paul's account.[1]

It is obvious from the outset that Paul is describing a meal and not just a liturgical act involving a little bread and wine. This is a full meal where drunkenness and gluttony are problems. Paul condemns the Christians for their lack of Christian unity and for the thoughtless selfishness which they manifest in their eating. They actually are profaning the body and blood of Christ. Ideally, the celebration of the Lord's Supper would commemorate Christ's crucifixion and resurrection, be a time of communion with the living Lord and an anticipation of Christ's victorious return to establish the messianic kingdom.[2] The Corinthians fail to see this significance in the Lord's Supper, and are judged by their very intemperance, an intemper-

[1] C. T. Craig, "The First Epistle to the Corinthians," *The Interpreter's Bible* (New York: Abingdon Press, 1953), X, 130.

[2] *Ibid.*, p. 145.

ance which may ultimately lead to a separating of the love feast from the liturgical act of the Lord's Supper.

Christ is the major difference between the Pauline interpretation of the Lord's Supper and the common meal of the sectarians. Paul urges the Corinthian Christians to commemorate Christ's death and at the same time eat as though the risen Christ is present with them. There is no comparable idea among the sectarians unless we accept the conjecture of Dupont-Sommer that the sectarians expected the return of their crucified leader and even then sensed that he was mystically present among them. Personally, I do not find a Pauline mysticism in the Dead Sea Scrolls, and am dubious if we should even describe the sectarian religion as a mystical religion. Certainly, the sectarian hope for the future resurrection of the Teacher of Righteousness was not the same as the Christian conviction that the risen Lord was present at the communion table.

Paul comes closest to Qumran thought when he teaches that the Lord's Supper points to the coming of the messianic age. We have already seen that the sectarian meal may have been an anticipation of the messianic banquet, but even here the Christians were one step ahead of the sectarians because they believed that their Lord had already been raised from the dead.

Moving to the Gospel According to Mark, we find Jesus blessing both the bread and the wine and giving thanks to God. This is in part a Eucharistic rite because the word "Eucharist" comes from a Greek word that means "to give thanks." (Paul also mentions the giving of thanks.) But more important, the Gospel notes the sacrificial quality of Jesus' life and calls upon the disciples to share with him this food, and perhaps even share whatever suffering may come to them until that day in the near future when they will all be together again in the Kingdom. The bread signifies Jesus' body, which will soon be given over to death. The cup of wine is a fitting symbol of Jesus' blood (and hence, in Jewish thought, his life) which will be "poured out for many." This cup of wine will also stand as a vivid reminder of the life and power of the Kingdom which is coming soon.

A. Powell Davies, the late minister of All Souls Unitarian Church in Washington, D. C., thought it "scarcely reasonable to question" the organic relationship between the Last Supper and the sectarian meal, but his own conjectures are far from convincing. There is, for instance, no textual basis in the Dead Sea Scrolls for the suggestion by Davies that the sectarians allowed the bread to represent the messiahs of Aaron and Israel. Nor is there any evidence in either Mark or Paul that Jesus identified himself with the "Messiah anticipated in the sacred meal of the Essenes." [3] It might be added that there is no suggestion in the Dead Sea Scrolls that the death of the Teacher of Righteousness had redemptive value. Jesus did bless the bread, as did the sectarian priest, but this practice of blessing food was so common in Judaism as to make this comparison of questionable significance, and it must also be remembered that Jesus was not a priest.

We cannot here go into a detailed study of the place of communion meals in Jewish worship, but I would suggest that the sectarian meal may have been similar to the meal eaten by ancient Hebrew priests at the sanctuary when a sacrifice was being offered to God. It should also be remembered that Melchizedek, the priest-king of Salem (pre-Israelite Jerusalem), blessed Abraham and shared bread and wine with him. It may be that both the sectarians and Jesus reflected Jewish customs of the Old Testament period and were organically related only to the extent that they both shared a common heritage.

Was the Jerusalem Church Like the Qumran Community?

Life in the Jerusalem church is described in the book of Acts. A group of believers came together and had all things in common. They sold their goods and possessions and distributed the community wealth according to the needs of the individual

[3] Cf. A. Powell Davies, *The Meaning of the Dead Sea Scrolls*, pp. 98 ff.

members. No one was hungry or in want in the Jerusalem church because they broke bread together and were greatly concerned about one another's needs. Their fellowship was further enriched by study and by prayer. They were grateful to God, who had called them out to be the true church. They were the elect who had been united and strengthened by the outpouring of the Holy Spirit, the elect who would remain faithful until the consummation of the new age which had already begun in the life, death, and resurrection of Christ.

The similarities between this kind of fellowship and community life at Qumran are obvious. Both were tightly knit groups of committed people who believed they had been elected by God to serve as the church, or true Israel. The promises of God had been made to them, promises which they believed were being fulfilled in their respective communities. Since the Messiah had already come, according to the convictions of the members of the Jerusalem church, their church stood in a later moment than did the Qumran community, which still looked forward to the coming of its messiahs, but both groups were filled with anticipation.

There may even be similarities in the actual organizational details of the two communities. The superintendent of Qumran may have performed many of the same functions that Peter performed in the Jerusalem community. At least, in the book of Acts, Peter challenged both Ananias and Sapphira when they lied about their wealth, and this was a function of the superintendent in the Manual of Discipline. It should also be noted in this connection that in both communities there were obvious penalties for lying about the amount of one's property.

Whether there was a special council of twelve men in both communities is open to question. My own preference is for a fifteen-man ruling body in Qumran and a twelve-man ruling group in the Jerusalem church. The three extra priests in the Qumran community were not found in the early church. Other students of the scrolls suggest that Peter, James, and John were the church's counterpart of the three priests in the Qumran community, but, as Burrows notes, none of these was a priest.

The differences between the church and the Qumran community are equally impressive. The sectarian community was a priestly organization committed to life in the wilderness in order to remain undefiled by the heretical interpretations of the law which were prevalent in Jerusalem. Women were either excluded entirely from the community, or at least played a minor role in its life. The sectarians were determined to keep their special knowledge secret from the wicked Jews who lived outside their organization. They were an exclusive group. There was no desire among them to mingle with the world and make converts from among all people. And, of course, there was no person in Qumran comparable to Jesus of Nazareth whose resurrection became the cornerstone of the emerging Christian community.

It is sometimes suggested that the Qumran community and the Jerusalem church were similar, in that both groups practiced baptism and ate common meals together. The inappropriateness of such a conclusion has already been noted in some detail.[4]

The same caution is in order when similarities are claimed on the basis that both communities spoke of themselves as being members of a new covenant. Father Graystone, a Roman Catholic priest and professor in England, may be correct when he suggests that the Qumran covenant was new only in the sense of being a renewal of the old Mosaic covenant. The book of Deuteronomy tells how Moses worked with the people of Israel to get them to renew their vows and reaffirm their intention of keeping the terms of the covenant. In Nehemiah, Ezra urges the people to repent of their sins and return to the covenant which God made with Abraham and Moses. In each of these instances,

[4] *Supra,* pp. 128-40.

the people regarded the law as the supreme revelation of God's will for his people.

Christians, on the other hand, regarded Christ as the supreme revelation of God's will for them. They did believe that they were members of the new covenant, and to this extent may have reflected the words in Jeremiah that a new covenant would be made with a people who had the law written upon their hearts. The Mosaic law was still valuable, but it was to be interpreted in terms of God's supreme revelation in Christ. There was a radical newness here which transcended the new covenant of Qumran. In a word, then, it was still the Christ-event which made the big difference between Qumran and the Jerusalem church.

Do the Scrolls Shed New Light on the Fourth Gospel?

Schubert, the Catholic scholar from the University of Vienna, says one of the most important results of research in the Dead Sea Scrolls is the discovery of evidence which proves conclusively the Jewish origin of the Fourth Gospel. For years, many interpreters of the New Testament have assigned a relatively late date to the Fourth Gospel because of their conviction that it reflected both Hellenic and Gnostic thought patterns. To give time for this non-Jewish influence to make itself felt, a post-first-century date has often been assigned to the final composition of the Fourth Gospel.

Now that we have the Dead Sea Scrolls, it is evident that some of the supposedly peculiar phrases of the Fourth Gospel were well known to other Jews who lived in Palestine at the time of Jesus. The light-darkness motif is found both in the Fourth Gospel and in the scrolls, as is the truth-error theme. Jesus' words to Nicodemus, that he must be born of water and the Spirit before he could enter the kingdom, may reflect the terminology of the Manual of Discipline, where it states that God will cleanse a man by a holy spirit, a cleansing which is like a water of purification. Certainly it is not difficult to find references to the children of light in both the War scroll and the Fourth Gospel.

While agreeing with Schubert that there is now new reason for emphasizing the Jewish origin of the Fourth Gospel, I would also agree with Rowley's view that Johannine theology is "poles asunder" from the theology of the scrolls. For while the logos doctrine (the Greek word *logos* appears in the first verse of the Gospel and is often translated as "word") owes more to a Jewish heritage than to Greek influence, the word which becomes flesh according to the Fourth Gospel has no counterpart in Judaism. The sectarians knew nothing of this incarnation theme which lies at the heart of Johannine thought, a theme which, along with the resurrection emphasis, distinguishes all New Testament thought from that found at Qumran.

IX

The Significance of the Scrolls

Is Christianity Threatened by the Discovery of the Scrolls?

PROFESSOR BURROWS OF YALE UNIVERSITY, A SCHOLAR WHO can scarcely be accused of being a dogmatic and narrow-minded Christian, says that after the first seven years of studying the Dead Sea Scrolls he did not find his understanding of the New Testament "substantially affected." In his second book on the Dead Sea Scrolls, Burrows adds the further observation that there is nothing in the Dead Sea Scrolls which disproves the basic tenets of Christianity as these are found in the historic statements of the faith.

Competent Jewish scholars lend support to the above conclusion. Theodor Gaster says,

It must be stated emphatically—particularly in view of recent exaggerated claims—that the Dead Sea Covenanters (or whatever we may choose to call this community) were in no sense Christians and held none of the fundamental theological doctrines of the Christian faith.[1]

Gaster elaborates this affirmation by saying that there is not a "shred or trace" in the Dead Sea Scrolls of the distinctive Christian doctrines that an incarnate Son died on a cross, saved

[1] T. H. Gaster, *The Dead Sea Scriptures*, pp. 18-19.

men from original sin by his passion, and was subsequently raised from the dead.

Samuel Sandmel, another Jewish scholar who has specialized in New Testament studies, expresses the same general feeling in even more pointed language. In the written report of Sandmel's presidential address to the Society of Biblical Literature and Exegesis for the year 1961, he suggests that his being Jewish may absolve him from any accusation that his theological predispositions prevent him from seeing the clear implications of the Dead Sea Scrolls for the future understanding of the New Testament and Christianity.[2] Admitting that the Christian religion owes much to Jewish and Greek houses of thought, Sandmel observes that Christianity also has unique stones in its edifice, stones "hewn out of truly original unprecedented Christian religious experience." He says that there is nothing in the Dead Sea Scrolls comparable to the Christology in the New Testament.

The actual evidence from the Qumran texts supports the conclusions of Burrows, Gaster, and Sandmel. The very silence of the Dead Sea Scrolls about the basic tenets of the Christian faith would seem to say something about the distinctive building blocks in the Christian religion. The resurrection of Jesus is stressed in the New Testament. He is a present and living Lord for the community of believers. The Fourth Gospel emphasizes the pre-existence of the Word who becomes incarnate in Jesus. Paul is a new man in Christ. Even more to the point, Jesus himself speaks and acts with an authority which is not found in the Teacher of Righteousness. The Teacher derives his authority from the Scriptures which he interprets. If Bornkamm of Heidleberg is correct, Jesus' authority is the immediate authority of one who knows that the will of God is being fulfilled moment by moment in his own life. These themes

---

[2] Samuel Sandmel, "Parallelomania," *Journal of Biblical Literature* LXXXI, Part I, (March, 1962), 1-13.

from the New Testament permeate Christianity; yet, curiously enough, they cannot be found in the Dead Sea Scrolls.

Moreover, many of the supposed similarities between sectarian doctrines and practices and those of the New Testament become more apparent than real when they are studied closely. The Lord's Supper in the New Testament commemorates the crucifixion and the resurrection of Jesus and points forward to the expected return of the Lord. The sectarian meals do not commemorate the death and resurrection of the Teacher of Righteousness. Nor is the Christian sacrament of baptism, performed once in the name of the risen Lord, much like the ritual washings at Qumran. It is also questionable if the priestly community of the sectarians isolated in the wilderness of Judea is actually very similar to the early Christian community in Jerusalem.

Those students of the scrolls who do feel that Christianity is being challenged by the discovery of the Dead Sea Scrolls may be misunderstanding the nature of the Christian religion. They may be assuming, for instance, that the value of Christianity depends directly upon Jesus' ability to present an original and unique system of ideas and universal truths. If this assumption is correct, it would indeed be a threat to Christianity to find its supposedly distinctive teachings already embodied in the literature of a Jewish sect which predated the Christian movement. If it is assumed that God's supposed self-revelation in Jesus must be authenticated in terms of Jesus' teaching alone, then this claim would seem to be jeopardized if comparable teachings and insights could be found among the sectarians.

As a matter of fact, many Christians would reject this interpretation of Christianity and claim that God's revelation came not so much in Jesus' teachings and ideas as in his life, death, and resurrection. Some of these Christians would not hesitate to admit that many of Jesus' teachings parallel those of earlier Jewish prophets, and they even go so far as to say that Jesus

147

was wrong when he preached that the kingdom of God would come soon. It may seem strange to the lay reader, but the fact is that many able Christian scholars and theologians are prepared to grant that Jesus' knowledge and ideas were limited and conditioned by the age in which he lived, while at the same time affirming with equal conviction that Jesus was the pre-existent Son of God who became incarnate, suffered, died on the cross, and was resurrected to rule over his church. This type of Christian certainly does not feel that the Dead Sea Scrolls present any threat to Christianity.

What Is the Significance of the Scrolls?

Fifteen years have elapsed since the scrolls were first found by Muhammad adh-Dhib. Thousands of books, articles, and notes have been published on the subject by biblical scholars and popular writers. This new wealth of information has not caused any radical or revolutionary change in our understanding of Christianity. Traditionalists have remained traditional in their outlook. Liberal theologians who are cautious and disciplined have not thought it proper to argue that there is any evidence from Qumran which will seriously alter the views of even the more conservative Christians. They recognize that the valuable information which comes to us from the Dead Sea Scrolls cannot prove or disprove the basic doctrines of traditional Christianity. Everyone, however, agrees that the scrolls have been, and continue to be, a significant discovery in terms of the new information which is now available as a result of their discovery.

First, these scrolls are significant because they provide information about the beliefs and organization of a sectarian group of Jews who were contemporaries with Jesus. Since Jesus was a Jew, it is important for every serious student of the Bible to know as much as possible about the Jews of this age. Prior to the discovery of the Dead Sea Scrolls, most of our information about the Judaism of this time came to us secondhand from the pens of men who reflected upon this period of history. Now, we have a wealth of written documents from which we can gain firsthand information about this age. The sectarian beliefs about God, election, messiahs, the two spirits, and the nature of man assume form within an apocalyptic framework of thought, and help us appreciate the variety of belief within the Judaism of the first two centuries B.C. and the first century of the Christian era.

Secondly, the Dead Sea Scrolls reveal much about the biblical texts we have been using. The St. Mark's Isaiah scroll, for instance, reassures us of the dependability of the Hebrew text which we have been using as a basis for our English translations. We go back in history one thousand years and discover that the Hebrew text of Isaiah known at Qumran does not differ appreciably from the Hebrew text of the late ninth or early tenth century. In spite of the human factor, devout and learned Jews can only be praised for the accuracy of the text which they preserved across the ages.

The Dead Sea Scrolls also suggest that the Greek translation of the Hebrew Bible must be taken seriously. This Greek translation, known as the "Septuagint" because of the tradition that seventy or seventy-two scholars prepared it, appears to represent accurately an underlying Hebrew tradition. This means that biblical scholars can now feel more justification for their decision to correct the Hebrew text by reference to the Greek text, especially if they are working on the text of the book of Samuel. This is true because texts of Samuel found at Qumran agree with the Septuagint rather than with the standard Masoretic text of the Hebrew Bible.

Thirdly, the Dead Sea Scrolls help date the original composition of many biblical books. It is now questionable whether any prophetic book, or even large portion of a prophetic book, was written later than the early second century B.C. The finding of fragments of the biblical book of Psalms and the Psalms scroll from Cave XI will probably make late dates for the psalms unlikely. Those who have dated certain psalms in the last century B.C. may now have to revise these dates. New Testament specialists are reconsidering the dates of composition for such New Testament works as the Fourth Gospel and the Pastoral epistles (I and II Timothy and Titus). The presence of a second-century B.C. Daniel manuscript at Qumran brings us back to within half a century of the time when the book was originally composed, and fragments of Ecclesiastes may once more open up the question of Greek influence in this particular work. No thorough treatment of either Old Testament literature or New Testament literature can ignore these new problems raised by the discovery of the Dead Sea Scrolls.

Occasionally, laymen ask if the Dead Sea Scrolls support the Protestant or the Catholic version of the Bible. What they really want to know is whether or not the "Bible" of the sectarians contained the so-called apocryphal books. To answer this question is to bring out a fourth contribution of the scrolls.

There is no proof that the sectarians had a definitely limited body of literature which they regarded as especially sacred, so their Bible can be spoken of in only a qualified sense. It is known that they were fond of Isaiah, Psalms, and the Law, to mention but three examples. Conversely, no examples of the books of Maccabees or Esther have been found at Qumran. It is also true that the sectarians had much literature which cannot be found in either a Catholic or a Protestant Bible, but it is uncertain whether they regarded all their literature as of equal inspiration and importance.

Paleographers find the Dead Sea Scrolls very significant because of the rich variety of scripts now available to them for comparative study and analysis. Prior to the discovery of the scrolls, there was very little inscribed material from this period of history. Now, guided by the dated texts from Murabbaat, the specialists can reconstruct the chronology of various peculiarities of the Hebrew script with sufficient precision to date some of the scrolls within twenty-five years of their actual date of writing. This may not seem like precision to the laymen, but it is certainly helpful for the student of ancient manuscripts.

Finally, the scrolls enable us to understand the development of the Hebrew and Aramaic languages during the first pre-Christian and first post-Christian centuries. The presence of vowel consonants (consonants which are missing in the vowelless text) in the Dead Sea Scrolls aids in the correct pronunciation of classical Hebrew. It also helps in studying the development and standardization of the consonantal text. Likewise, the Aramaic of the Genesis Apocryphon is valuable because it sheds light upon Palestinian Aramaic used during the time of Jesus. Jesus, of course, spoke the Aramaic language.

Thus we see that while the Dead Sea Scrolls neither threaten Christianity nor revolutionize our understanding of this religion, their importance is so great that specialists will be busy for years assimilating and relating this new body of information to their respective disciplines. All who value new information about the Bible and the people who produced it will be permanently indebted to the sectarians and their scrolls, a bedouin boy and a lost goat, and the host of scholars who interpret these discoveries for us.

X

A Scientific Postscript

*Are Scientific Methods Utilized
by Scholars in Scrolls Research?*

FORTUNATELY FOR STUDENTS OF RELIGION, THE BLIND AND impassioned dogmatism of the past is past if not forgotten. If Libby can help scholars date the linen cloth found in Cave I by radiocarbon methods, they are eager to avail themselves of his services and grateful for his findings. If the latest techniques in infrared photography can make more legible the obscure writing on a Dead Sea Scroll, they shall certainly use this modern method. If a specialist in the art of handling ancient leathers can unroll a scroll without damaging its hidden script, they marvel at his skill and turn to him for advice about handling the thousands of fragments which come from the caves in the wilderness of Judea. If an electronic computer made by IBM can both index the scrolls and make predictions about what Hebrew letters should be supplied in the portions of the Dead Sea Scrolls where the text is missing, experts are delighted to accept the helping hand, even though it be electronic.

It should also be remembered that biblical scholars have been using their own scientific methods in biblical research. The best biblical scholars are combination linguists, archaeologists, historians, textual critics, and theologians. It is not uncommon for a biblical scholar to be able to read seven or eight different languages, and many specialists can read ten or more languages with considerable facility.

The archaeologist can study the clay or paste from which jars are made and begin to form a conclusion about the age of the jars. The curves of the jar, the texture of the clay, the design of the mouth and base, and any markings which appear on the jar provide additional clues for the specialist. If coins are found in the same strata with the jars, the dating becomes even more certain. The material used in the making of implements is also an indication of stone-age, bronze-age, or iron-age artisans. We have already seen that this kind of archaeological evidence is available to the student of the Dead Sea Scrolls.

The biblical student must at least be enough of a historian to know something of the life and culture of the Sumerians, the Babylonians, the Assyrians, the Persians, the Greeks, and the Romans. If he is also an Egyptologist, so much the better. Add to this a knowledge of the Canaanites and their religion, and assume that any biblical student worthy of the name is familiar with the history of Israel and the history of the Christian church, and one can begin to sense that scientific investigation has not eluded biblical specialists. It is too much to hope that any one man can be expert in all these fields, but it is interesting to note that many of the more cautious interpretations of the Dead Sea Scrolls come from men who have proved their ability in several of these areas.

Textual critics study scriptures with the hope of providing us with as accurate a text as is possible. They know that there are literally hundreds of Bibles and texts and that these texts do not all agree. It is their responsibility to compare and evaluate the diverse readings, group them into families, tell us about the place and date of their origin, and make their suggestions as to which of these readings reflects most accurately the thought of the original author. These textual critics are the ones who will compare the new biblical texts from Qumran with existing texts to see whether more can be learned about the origin of our Bible.

Finally, there is a scientific method in theology. Guided by the textual critics and linguists who tell him what the ancients said, the theologian attempts to re-create the psychological dispositions and cultural influences which have helped shape the confessions of biblical man. He compares biblical thought with the thought of the ancient Near East and then attempts to communicate the biblical thought to the modern reader. Hopefully, his choice of words will be precise and his presentation orderly. He compares the biblical thought with modern philosophies and points out the parallels and contrasts, all the while knowing that his own efforts will inevitably bear the stamp of his own subjectivism. But the very recognition by the theologian that his system is just another human formulation warns everyone that theologies are not sacrosanct, certain guides to the mysteries of God. Theologies come and go. Only God is eternal.

What Is Radiocarbon Dating?

Radiocarbon dating is the process of determining the age of samples submitted for testing by measuring the amount of radioactive carbon (carbon 14) therein. Credit for the development of this process goes to Willard F. Libby, who is now professor of chemistry at the University of California at Los Angeles and Director of the Institute of Geophysics and Planetary Physics. Whereas a complete knowledge of this process has been sufficient to win a Nobel prize for Libby, the essence of the theory is simple enough to be explained to the lay reader.

The process of producing radioactive carbon begins in outer space with the very same cosmic rays which are a matter of concern for all future astronauts. These cosmic rays impinge upon atoms in the upper atmosphere, thereby freeing neutrons, which in turn transmute the nitrogen of the atmosphere into the radioactive carbon that is eventually found mixed with the ordinary carbon dioxide breathed in by plants. Animals that eat these plants will also accumulate a supply of radioactive carbon.

As long as plants and animals remain alive, they continue to take in this radioactive carbon, but as soon as they die, the process of ingestion ceases and the relatively unstable radiocarbon begins to disintegrate. In 5,568 years about one half the original amount of carbon 14 will have disappeared and one half will remain. Fortunately, nuclear chemists know that the original ratio of radioactive carbon to normal carbon is one to a trillion. In other words, if the living organism at its death contains one trillion atoms of ordinary carbon, the nuclear chemist would expect to find just one atom of radioactive carbon. Knowing this original ratio and given the half-life of radioactive carbon (the half-life is that period of time required for the disintegration of one half the original amount of carbon 14), the researcher can take his Geiger counter and determine the ratio of radiocarbon to ordinary carbon in his sample and then calculate the date of his sample.

Perhaps an example will make this process clearer. A researcher takes the sample to be dated and burns it to release both the radioactive carbon dioxide and the normal carbon dioxide. If the researcher has collected ten trillion molecules of ordinary carbon dioxide in his sample, he would know that at the point when the organism died there were ten molecules of radioactive carbon dioxide present in this sample. If he discovers that only five molecules of radioactive carbon dioxide remain, he will conclude that the sample is 5,568 years old.

Of even more interest to the reader is the actual use of the radiocarbon dating in establishing the age of some linen cloth found in Cave I at Qumran. According to the records of Professor Libby, which he has graciously checked for me, about two ounces of linen cloth were submitted to him on November 14, 1950, by Carl Kraeling of the Oriental Institute of the University of Chicago. Libby, who was at that time associated with the University of Chicago's Institute for Nuclear Studies, burned about one ounce of this linen cloth on December 8, 1950, and measured its age on December 19 and 20 of this same year.

Libby's calculations showed that an average age for this material was 1,917 years, with a possible error of plus or minus two hundred years. In other words, an average date for the linen cloth would be A.D. 33, but the margin of error was such that the cloth might be dated as early as 168 B.C. (there being no year zero) or as late as A.D. 233. There is even one chance in three that none of these were correct—Gordon Fergusson, who is now associated with Libby, pointed this out to me in an interview—but in spite of these uncertainties Libby's work tended to confirm the evidence of archaeology and paleography that the scrolls and jars of Cave I are ancient, and not medieval as Zeitlin thinks.

Zeitlin, of course, stresses the unreliability of radiocarbon dating, but continuing experiments tend to confirm the general reliability of the process. A test of an Acacia wooden beam of known age (4,650 years) produced a reading of 3,979 plus or minus 350 years. A test on the wood from the deck of an Egyptian funerary ship known to be about 3,750 years old produced an average date of 3,631 plus or minus 180 years.

In a recent telephone conversation with Libby I learned that with the improved techniques which are now used, as little as one ounce of material could yield a date that would be correct within a period of one hundred years. Since Libby and his colleagues do this dating without charge to the extent that their time and energy permits, one almost wishes that Israel or Jordan would part with one ounce of the material so that a test could be made of the age of the leathers used in some of the Qumran scrolls. Of course, there is the possibility that both ancient linen and ancient material can be used for scrolls of relatively recent vintage, but the gradual accumulation of evidence for the antiquity of the scrolls might convince some skeptics.[1]

What Is Infrared Photography?

Infrared photography employs a special film which enables the camera eye to see things the human eye cannot see. As early as A.D. 1800, Sir William Herschel, an organist turned astronomer, discovered infrared radiation. Using a prism, Sir William refracted ordinary sunlight and measured with a thermometer the heat-radiating capacity of the various visible light rays in the spectrum. But more important, he discovered heat radiation produced by the longer-than-red wavelengths which were invisible to the human eye. He had discovered what we now call infrared radiation.[2]

Infrared wavelengths are so long that the human eye cannot detect them (still, they are so short that it would be necessary to link more than 29,000 of them end to end to cover a distance of one inch), but infrared film is sensitive to these infrared waves. For this reason, a camera using infrared film can photograph a flatiron in the dark. Or, in similar fashion, a flatiron could be used to supply the needed illumination to take pictures of other objects in an otherwise darkened room.

The uses of infrared photography are many and varied. Police departments can use infrared techniques to bring out otherwise invisible stains on clothing, to read a signature or an address which has been obliterated by a dye-type ink, to photograph fingerprints on a piece of charred paper, and to reveal more clearly the bruises on the human body. Occasionally, infrared

[1] Cf. W. F. Libby's book, *Radiocarbon Dating* (2nd ed.: Chicago: The University of Chicago Press, 1955), pp. 77 ff., for a listing of the examples used above. While much of Libby's book is too technical for the lay reader, there are parts of the first chapter which do explain the formation of radiocarbon in terms understandable to the neophyte. See also the article by Edward S. Deevey, Jr., "Radiocarbon Dating," *Scientific American*, CLXXXVI (February, 1952), 24-28.

[2] Cf. Bryce Crawford, Jr., "Chemical Analysis by Infrared," *Scientific American*, CLXXXIX (October, 1953), 42-48.

photography is used to take pictures in the dark of an unsuspecting burglar. In such instances the criminal will not know that he is being photographed because there will be no flash of visible light. Medical doctors can use infrared photography to study certain human veins, because infrared film is not sensitive to oxygenated blood but is sensitive to nonoxygenated blood in the veins. This penetrating quality of infrared film is valuable in certain types of aerial photography, and is sometimes used by amateur photographers who wish to penetrate the haze and get a clearer, more detailed picture of the terrain.[3]

Infrared techniques have been used to read some of the script of the Dead Sea Scrolls. F. B. Adams, Jr., Director of the Pierpont Morgan Library in New York City, informs me in a personal letter that Sukenik brought undecipherable sections of the Dead Sea Scrolls to that library in 1949. Mr. Adams says, "We made infrared photographs of them in order to reveal the writing that was under the smears of bitumen. The results were entirely successful." This success was probably due to the fact that the carbon ink of the scrolls absorbed more of the infrared light than did the surrounding leather of the scrolls. This increased absorption of infrared light produced a corresponding increase in the temperature of the script, which in turn photographed better on infrared film.

According to F.M. Cross of Harvard, all the fragments which were brought into the Palestine Archaeological Museum were photographed with infrared film. If the leather was exceedingly dark, exposures of more than an hour's duration were made, but under normal conditions six to eight minutes' exposure was sufficient to produce readable prints.

Had these scrolls been discovered one hundred years earlier,

[3] The uses of infrared photography and ultraviolet film (which has also been used in the photographing of the Dead Sea Scrolls) are described in a Kodak data booklet. I had access to the fourth edition of this booklet, titled *Infrared and Ultraviolet Photography*. These booklets are made available by the Eastman Kodak Company of Rochester, New York.

the scholars would have had difficulty reading some of the script. Now, due to the modern science of infrared photography, the scholars can see through the dirt and discoloration of the leather and read again a script that was written more than two thousand years ago.

How Has IBM Helped in Scrolls Research?

An IBM 705 electronic computer has prepared an index of some of the nonbiblical scrolls from Qumran. A news release prepared by the IBM World Trade Corporation for March 27, 1958, explains that almost 30,000 words have already been placed upon IBM cards, one word per card, and that these cards show not only the word but its exact location in the original Dead Sea Scroll from which it has been taken. Thus, the researcher who wants to know how often the words "Teacher of Righteousness" occur in the Habakkuk Commentary can now turn to the alphabetically arranged lists which have been printed in Hebrew by the 705's printing unit. The appropriate list will not only show the researcher how often the phrase occurs but will also indicate the exact column and line in which the phrase is found.

But the IBM 705 can do even more! As it electronically records the information which has been punched into the IBM cards, it builds up the capacity to analyze style of writing and make a prediction on the basis of mathematical probability as to whether the style has changed, thereby suggesting an editorial hand. In cases where words are missing from a given scroll, the 705, knowing the writer's style, can predict what words should be placed in the gap. Just to check their brain child at this point, the operators purposely deleted portions of a familiar text and then fed the resulting incomplete text into the machine. It was found that the 705 could replace correctly as many as five consecutive words.

This does not mean that the study of theology and literary creativity can be reduced to mathematical probabilities and statistics. It *does* mean that an electronic computer can take hours of drudgery out of scrolls research. Ten men and an IBM 705 can index all the works of Thomas Aquinas in five years. It has been estimated that it would take fifty scholars forty years to do this same job without the IBM.[4]

How Do the Scholars Handle and Identify the Fragments of the Scrolls?

As many a layman has remarked, piecing together scroll fragments is like working out a jigsaw puzzle. Remembering that there are hundreds of manuscripts represented at Qumran by thousands of fragments, the lay person is sure to marvel at the patience of the members of the scroll team who collected the jagged pieces into their respective manuscripts before transcribing, translating, and publishing the results of their particular puzzles.

Actually, the task is not quite so impossible as the layman suspects. The trained member of the international team of scholars whose job it was to prepare all these fragments for publication soon became expert in identifying the handwriting of the scribe whose scroll he was trying to reconstruct. As he walked about the scrollery, peering through the glass plates at the fragments, he would catch a glimpse of a distinctive ligature or peculiarity of style which matched that of his scribe. Checking the texture of the material and comparing its color with other fragments which he had already found, the scholar might guess that he had found another piece to his particular puzzle. He was not always right, but usually he was, and his manuscript began to take shape.

Prior to this hunting process, the fragments had to be cleaned and often humidified before the leather became soft and pliable enough to be flattened for preservation between the glass plates. If a brushing did not remove deeply ingrained dust, it might be necessary to take a camel's-hair brush and apply a thin film

[4] *New York Times*, September 28, 1956.

of a nonacid oil such as castor oil to the fragment. This oil made the white dust translucent, thus enabling the scholar to read the writing underneath. If humidification was necessary, the fragments were placed in humidifiers which contained glycerin and water. If the relative humidity was kept above 70 per cent for a period of eighteen to twenty hours, even the more difficult pieces softened and became pliable.

There is, of course, no scientific method for restoring the portions of the texts which have been eaten by worms or completely lost to the weathering process, but cracked pieces can be reinforced and warped pieces can be flattened so that grouping and identification can proceed. Cross reports that by the summer of 1956 only twenty odd plates of unidentified fragments remained in the scrollery. This is certainly a tribute to the skill and perseverance of the scroll team.

One of the easiest tasks is that of identifying a fragment of a biblical scroll. If the scroll researcher can make out one or two words on the fragment, he can check a concordance of Hebrew words in the Bible to see if these same words appear in the Bible. (A concordance is a book which lists every word in the Bible in alphabetical order, telling just where in the Bible this particular word can be found.) If so, he may guess that he has a biblical fragment. If he has portions of several lines or portions of more than one column, there is no difficulty at all in identifying the exact biblical passage represented by the fragments. The identification of nonbiblical and sectarian works poses more difficult problems, but even here the members of the international team learned to move with such skill that they could recognize a member of their puzzle family while engaged in a friendly conversation with a visitor. As is always the case, the experts make the difficult look easy.

Appendix

Have More Scrolls Been Found in Israel?

More scrolls and documents have been found in Israel during 1960 and 1961. Whereas these documents will probably never be included as part of the Dead Sea Scrolls, they are sufficiently important to be considered here.

In the spring of 1960, a small army of Israeli searchers set out to look for more scrolls and treasures in the cliff caves of modern Israel. These caves are located just west of the Dead Sea and immediately south of the present Israeli-Jordanian border. Aided by aerial reconnaissance, which provided detailed pictures of the face of the cliffs to be investigated, the plucky Israeli students and farmers who had volunteered for this expedition embarked upon their hazardous search. Sometimes a scout, supported only by a rope attached to a Jeep, would dangle in mid-air over a cliff as he studied a given cave. At other times, rope ladders fashioned under the watchful eye of a navy knot expert, who had joined the expedition for precisely this purpose, provided the entrance to otherwise inaccessible caves.

Much of the material contained in this appendix is included in another article by the author in *Together* (title and facts of publication not yet known), and is used here in slightly different form by permission of the editors of *Together*. At the time of this writing, the primary source of information about the Israeli explorations is *The Expedition to the Judean Desert, 1960*. This publication is a revised edition of the original Hebrew publication which appeared in the *Bulletin of the Israeli Exploration Society*, 25, 1961. Cf. also articles by Yigael Yadin in the *Jerusalem Post*, May 20, 1960, and September 10, 1961.

As the Israelis explored these caves, they found ample evidence that the caves had been inhabited and used by men who lived in the Chalcolithic Age about four thousand years before the Christian Era, but the most spectacular finds were made by members of Yigael Yadin's crew as they explored a mammoth cave on the northern slope of the Wadi Hever. Pinhas Prutzky, one of Yadin's crew, crawled through a narrow passageway which led off from the third and deepest chamber of this cave, and to his shock found a collection of human skulls and bones. Yadin believes these to be the remains of men, women, and children who either starved to death or were killed when the Jews led by Bar Kokheba engaged in a second Jewish revolt against Rome in A.D. 132-35. The remains of a Roman campsite on top of the cliff seem to confirm Yadin's view that this area was under siege for a considerable period of time.

Of more direct interest to students of the Dead Sea Scrolls are the biblical fragments which the Israelis have discovered. Professor Aharoni's crew found fragments of the thirteenth chapter of the biblical book of Exodus. One of these parchment fragments contains a text that is identical with the Masoretic text, while the other fragment bears a variant reading which is not found in the Masoretic text but is found in the Greek (Septuagint) translation of the Torah.

On Sunday morning, April 3, 1960, a member of the Yadin crew found a parchment fragment of the book of Psalms. This fragment is roughly two inches square, and contains seven lines of script that clearly identify it as a portion of Psalm 15 and the beginning of Psalm 16. A definite margin between these two psalms shows that the ancient division of these two chapters corresponds exactly with that division in our modern Bibles. Yadin dates the writing of this parchment to the second half of the first century A. D. If his date is correct, this is obviously additional evidence and material for dating the scripts of the original Dead Sea Scrolls. Yadin is convinced that the script of this Psalms fragment is later than that used in most of the Dead Sea Scrolls but definitely earlier than that found in the biblical fragments of the Bar Kokheba period which have come from the Wadi Murabbaat.

On this same Sunday morning, another member of the Yadin

crew discovered a collection of letters written by Bar Kokheba to two men named Yehonatan and Masabala. Fourteen of these letters are on papyrus, and one is on wood. At least eight of the letters are written in the Aramaic language, four are in Hebrew, and two are in Greek. The letters deal with such matters as a threatened punishment for anyone failing to obey the commands of Bar Kokheba, instructions for Yehonatan, and complaints that Yehonatan and Masabala are not supporting Bar Kokheba's insurrection as fully as they might. While these letters have no direct connection with the sectarian Jews who produced the Dead Sea Scrolls, they do provide examples of handwriting of known age which will enable the specialist to date the script of the scrolls with greater precision. The Bar Kokheba letters are, of course, valuable in their own right because they reveal more about this leader of the Jewish revolt against Rome in the second century A. D.

During the period of March 14-27, 1961, a second Israeli expedition returned to the Wadi Hever. Again, it was Yadin's group which succeeded in discovering more than forty additional inscribed documents and letters in the very same Cave of the Letters which had been so fruitful in 1960. Some of these documents have not yet been published, but a preliminary study indicates that these bundles of papyrus and parchment documents will include such items as a contract for the lease of land by Bar Kokheba and statements about the method of taxation and rents which prevailed during the period of the second Jewish revolt. There is at least one marriage contract and yet another papyrus which discusses the problem of guardianship for an orphan.

In the *Jerusalem Post* for March 24, 1961, there is a report that Yadin found the first complete parchment scroll to have come down to us from the Roman period. We do not have any further information on this report and will have to wait for the official publication of the discoveries made by the expedition to the Wadi Hever in 1961.

Bibliography

Note: Thousands of books, articles, reviews, and notes have now been written about the scrolls. Rather than present an extensive list of these works, I shall cite here only those books which have been used as direct sources within the body of this book. Quotations from articles have been documented fully in the footnotes and will not be listed in the bibliography. For the reader who may be interested in a more detailed bibliography, I recommend the bibliographical entries which may be found in the two works by Millar Burrows listed below.

Allegro, J. M. *The Dead Sea Scrolls*. Harmondsworth: Penguin Books Ltd., 1956.

———. *The Treasure of the Copper Scroll*. Garden City, New York: Doubleday & Co., 1960.

Avigad, N., and Yadin, Y. *A Genesis Apocryphon*. Jerusalem: The Magnes Press of The Hebrew University and Heikhal ha-Sefer, 1956.

Barthélemy, D., and Milik, J. T. *(Qumran Cave I)*, *Discoveries in the Judean Desert I*. Oxford: Clarendon Press, 1955.

Burrows, M. *The Dead Sea Scrolls*. New York: The Viking Press, 1955.

———. *More Light on the Dead Sea Scrolls*. New York: The Viking Press, 1958.

Cross, F. M., Jr. *The Ancient Library of Qumran and Modern Biblical Studies*. Revised edition; Garden City, New York: Doubleday & Co., 1961.

Dupont-Sommer, A. *Die Essenischen Schriften Vom Toten Meer*. Translated by Walter W. Müller. Tübingen: J. C. B. Mohr (Paul Siebeck), 1960. An English translation of this book by G. Vermes is now available in paperback (Meridian) under the title *The Essene Writings from Qumran*.

———. *The Dead Sea Scrolls*. Translated by E. Margaret Rowley. New York: The Macmillan Company, 1952.

————. *The Jewish Sect of Qumran and the Essenes.* Translated by R. D. Barnett. New York: The Macmillan Company, 1956.

Gaster, T. H. *The Dead Sea Scriptures in English Translation.* Garden City, New York: Doubleday & Co., 1956.

Milik, J. T. *Ten Years of Discovery in the Wilderness of Judea.* Translated by J. Strugnell. London: S. C. M. Press, 1959.

Potter, C. F. *The Lost Years of Jesus Revealed.* Greenwich, Conn.: Fawcett Publications, Inc., 1958.

Sukenik, E. L., editor. *The Dead Sea Scrolls of The Hebrew University.* Jerusalem: The Magnes Press of The Hebrew University, 1955.

Wilson, E. *The Scrolls from the Dead Sea.* New York: Meridian Books, Inc., 1959.

Yadin, Y. *The Message of the Scrolls.* New York: Simon & Schuster, 1957.

Zeitlin, S. *The Dead Sea Scrolls and Modern Scholarship.* "The Jewish Quarterly Review Monograph Series, No. III" Philadelphia: Dropsie College, 1956.

Index